Lake Tahoe Bouldering

Lake Tahoe Bouldering

by Kevin Swift
and Chris McNamara

Published by
SuperTopo
2 Bradford Way
Mill Valley, CA 94941
www.supertopo.com

Written by Kevin Swift and Chris McNamara
Photos by Chris McNamara (unless otherwise noted)
Edited by Steve McNamara, Chris McNamara, DeAnne Musolf
Layout by Chris McNamara
Assistant layout by Clair Nicholas

Cover Photo: Kevin Swift at South Bliss. *Photo by Chris McNamara*
Cover Horizontal Photo: Emerald Bay scenic. *Photo by David Safanda*
Back Cover Photo: Mark Nicholas on Oak Tree in My Way Traverse (V8) at The Secrets. *Photo by Chris McNamara*
Contents photo: Kevin Swift bouldering at Grouse Slabs. *Photo by Chris McNamara*

Cover Design
by David Safanda, David Safanda Design Solutions. www.safanda.com

Swift, Kevin
Lake Tahoe Bouldering: SuperTopos

Contents

Warning!

Climbing is an inherently dangerous sport in which severe injuries or death may occur. Relying on the information in this book may increase the danger.

When climbing you can only rely on your skill, training, experience, and conditioning. **If you have any doubts as to your ability to safely climb any route in this guide, do not try it.**

This book is neither a professional climbing instructor nor a substitute for one. **It is not an instructional book. Do not use it as one.** It contains information that is nothing more than a compilation of opinions about bouldering in Lake Tahoe. **These opinions are neither facts nor promises.** Treat the information as opinions and nothing more. Do not substitute these opinions for your own common sense and experience.

Assumption of Risk

There may be errors in this book resulting from the mistake of the authors and/or the people with whom they consulted. The information was gathered from a variety of sources, which may not have been independently verified. Those who provided the information may have made mistakes in their descriptions. The authors may have made mistakes in their conveyance of the information in this book. **The authors cannot, therefore, guarantee the correctness of any of the information contained in this book.** The topographical maps, photo-diagrams, difficulty ratings, protection ratings, approach and/or descent information, suggestions about equipment, and other matters may be incorrect or misleading. Fixed protection may be absent, unreliable, or misplaced. **You must keep in mind that the information in this book may be erroneous, so use your own judgement when choosing, approaching, climbing, or descending from a route described in this book.**

DO NOT USE THIS BOOK UNLESS YOU [AND YOUR ESTATE] PROMISE NEVER TO TRY TO SUE US IF YOU GET HURT OR KILLED.

Disclaimer of Warranties

THE AUTHORS AND PUBLISHER WARN THAT THIS BOOK CONTAINS ONLY THE AUTHOR'S OPINIONS ON THE SUBJECTS DISCUSSED. THEY MAKE NO OTHER WARRANTIES, EXPRESSED OR IMPLIED, OF MERCHANTABILITY, FITNESS FOR PURPOSE, OR OTHERWISE, AND IN ANY EVENT, THEIR LIABILITY FOR BREACH OF ANY WARRANTY OR CONTRACT WITH RESPECT TO THE CONTENT OF THIS BOOK IS LIMITED TO THE PURCHASE PRICE OF THE BOOK. THEY FURTHER LIMIT TO SUCH PURCHASE PRICE THEIR LIABILITY ON ACCOUNT OF ANY KIND OF NEGLIGENT BEHAVIOR WHATSOEVER ON THEIR PART WITH RESPECT TO THE CONTENTS OF THIS BOOK.

Acknowledgements

The following folks contributed beta, feedback, topos, photos, and support. Thank you!

Justin Bailie
Dana Benson
Jesse Bonin
Derek Bloomquist
Warren Digness
Fitz Cahill
Shane Carigan
Tommy Caldwell
Scott Chandler
Paul Crawford
Matthew Delheimer
Mike Eadington
Stuart Emerson
Robin de la Fuente
David Fichter
Dave Goodwyn
Brad Goya
Dave Hatchett
Tom Herbert
Michael Keane
Matt Keebler
Jason Kuchnicki
Frank Lucido
Kay McNamara
Morgan McNamara
Steve McNamara
Sasha Musso
DeAnne Musolf
Kim Miller
The Nicholas Family: Mark,
    RuthEllen, Clair, Madelyn, Joe,
    Logan, Max, Ellie, Elaina, Danny, Harrison

Todd Offenbacher
Mike Ousley
Todd Paige
Beth Rodden
Corey Rich
Dustin Sabo
Brooke Sandahl
David Safanda
Jay Sell
Randy Spurrier
Andy Vaughan
Eric Volz
Tom Wright

Preface

What sets Tahoe apart is not just the number of boulders, it is the variety. You can climb Joshua Tree style rock by the lake or climb Yosemite-esque holds in the forest or drive 30 minutes east to the desert and climb impeccable volcanic pockets. It's all here, it's yearround, and even this book, the most complete coverage yet on the subject, can only whet your appetite.

This is Lake Tahoe's first bouldering guide. Initially, author Kevin Swift and I were excited about doing the inside tour of Lake Tahoe's boulders with Tahoe's most accomplished and active boulderers. But at first it was slim pickings. We started to wonder if there were actually enough boulder problems to fill a book.

But a few months into the project everything changed...drastically. Boulders started showing up everywhere. Often when a local showed us a new concentration, there were even more boulders close by that they hadn't climbed yet. Suddenly we had a new challenge: there were just too many boulders to document! To make matters worse, we became afflicted with the first ascent bug. We wanted to put up even more problems and pump up the load of documentation even more. Would it never end? Finally we had to say, "Enough is enough!" So every area listed in this guide has even more established problems than what we list. We were just not able to document them all. That gives you a great opportunity: Take a wrong turn while driving to one of the areas and you might find a first ascent waiting for you.

We can definitely use your help with beta on new problems for the next edition. We always want feedback on our books. Because this is the first guidebook to Lake Tahoe bouldering, we especially need your help. Send me an email if you find something you think should be included next time around. Also, if you know the name of a problem in the book that we weren't been able to identify, please email the name to us.

Lastly, we know that many of the ratings may be a little off. There just wasn't time to get a consensus rating on everything.

Chris McNamara
chris@supertopo.com

Introduction

By Kevin Swift

Granite, GRANITE, GRANITE! That's Tahoe in a nutshell. Not just any granite, either. Super quality, compact, weathered Sierra granite unfolds in every conceivable shape, size, and location. On almost any given day, you can roll into Tahoe from any direction and be pulling down within half an hour. There are boulders on ridgetops with endless views, and boulders lying in shadowy creek beds. There are boulders in forest and desert settings, exposed to the sun or hiding in shade, up high and down low, right in town, and half an hour up remote hillsides.

Everything from lie-down starts under low roofs to terrifying, guaranteed-death highballs, VB to V12, knob pimping, sloper slapping, slab teetering, crack jamming, edge cranking madness abounds. You'll die before you do all the problems around Lake Tahoe—one because your forearms will explode, two because you'll never find them all, and three because there isn't a person on Earth who can muster the necessary stoke to clean and tick every one of the thousands of untouched boulders splashed all over Tahoe even if they could find them.

This place will still be going off ten years from now, when people who are actually willing to hike for an hour finally come to town and start pillaging all the more remote potential. You simply can't go wrong here, and if you do manage to send everything in the guidebook, you will have lived here long enough to become a local and get a free pass to all the developing stuff we couldn't include without getting killed.

A word of caution is in order here, for all of you who still have jobs, significant others, and homes elsewhere. I've met a

Chris Ewing at the Momma Cat Boulder.

startling number of people who visited Tahoe for a week's vacation and are still here—two, five, or ten years later. I'm one of them. I came here just to check it out and after two years can't see living anywhere else for the moment. Maybe when I've worn the place out I'll want to leave, but that will take a while.

SuperTopo.com

All the Tahoe information below is available at www.supertopo.com with links directly to the sources for easier trip planning.

When to climb

The general Tahoe bouldering season is May-November. October and (a dry) November usually have the best conditions. In the summer, you generally want to seek the shade. The areas that are climbable all winter long are listed in the sidebar on page 13. During a lean snow year, boulder the areas in this book that are near a plowed road.

Getting There

Car Travel
A car is essential in Tahoe because public transportation is scarce. From San Francisco, drive Interstate 80 to Sacramento. For North Lake areas, continue on Interstate 80. For South Lake Areas, take Highway 50 east. Access all climbing areas in this guide off Highway 50, Highway 89, or Interstate 80.

Air Travel
Reno/Tahoe Airport is about an hour and fifteen minutes drive to South Lake Tahoe and Sacramento International Airport is about two hours away. You can also fly into Oakland or San Francisco, rent a car and drive about three hours.

Camping

There are hundreds of campsites in Tahoe. View the overview maps on pages 18-19 to locate these campsites. A great web site that lists many South and North Lake Tahoe camping areas is: www.explorer1.com/tahoe/camping.htm Fire permits are required for fires at many areas. For a list of ranger stations from which to get a fire permit: visit: www.fs.fed.us/r5/tahoe/

South Lake Free Camping

Phantom Spires

Camping is conveniently located at the Phantom Spires parking lot, along the logging road, and along Wright's Lake Road. It's all Forest Service land so you can camp just about anywhere. There are three large pullouts along the logging road that each accommodate four to eight cars. The first two have nice views but are often windy. The last pullout, the Phantom Spires parking area, is the largest and most wind-sheltered. There is also a great camping spot at the end of a 4WD road that leads to just below Lizard Head. There are no facilities so bring your own water. Bury your poop at least six inches underground. Be careful when building a fire. Build a tall fire ring and keep fires small.

Lover's Leap

Seconds from the boulders, the campground has all the necessities: picnic tables, pit toilets, privacy, drinking water, and a bar within a five minute walk. The 30 campsites have two to four tents sites each and come with one parking spot. Park additional cars on Highway 50. Each site also has a plastic storage bin for food storage (bring a padlock if storing valuables). Rangers enforce the 14 total days per year limit with fines. Carry out all your trash and dump it at the Strawberry Lodge for a fee or hunt in South Lake Tahoe for a dumpster. The Strawberry Lodge offers

---

Introductory Areas

These areas all have problems in the VB-V1 range:

The Secrets
Lovers Leap
Old County
Grouse Slab
Echo View
Washoe Boulders

---

showers or baths for $5. Each site has a campfire ring, and you should bring your own wood as the Forest Service discourages collecting locally.

Strawberry Tract Road/ The Secrets

Drive to 42 Mile Tract Road, the first left west of Strawberry Lodge. After you pass over the bridge over Strawberry Creek you can camp just about anywhere.

South Lake Tahoe Pay Camping

D.L. Bliss California State Park

Highway 89, South Lake Tahoe, CA (530) 525-7277. www.parks.ca.gov/default. asp?page_id=505

Fallen Leaf Lake

Highway 89, South Lake Tahoe, CA (530) 544-5994. www.fs.fed.us/r5/ltbmu/ recreation/camping/flcamp.shtml

Campground by the Lake

1150 Rufus Allen Blvd., South Lake Tahoe, CA (530) 542-6096. http://www. recreationintahoe.com/campground.htm

South Lake Restaurants

Thai: Orchid Thai, 2180 Lake Tahoe Blvd., (530) 544-5541
Burgers: Izzie's Burger Spa, 2591 Lake Tahoe Blvd., (530) 544-5030
Pizza: Bob Dog's Pizza, 3141 US Highway 50, (530) 577-2364
Mexican: The Cantina, Highway 89 and 10th St., (530) 544-1233
Chinese: Hunan Garden, 900 Emerald Bay Rd., (530) 544-5868
Seafood: The Chart House, 392 Kingsbury Grade, (775) 588-6276
Breakfast: Ernie's, 1146 Emerald Bay Rd., (530) 541-2161
Bar/Music: Divided Sky, 3200 US Highway 50, (530) 577-0775
Lunch: Sprouts, 3123 Harrison Avenue, (530) 541-6969.
Coffee: Alpina Café (free wireless), 822 Emerald Bay Rd., (530) 541-7449 or Alpen Sierra (free wireless), 3940 Lake Tahoe Blvd., Suite 1 (530) 544-7740

North Lake Restaurants

If you're brave and ready for the ultimate greasy spoon experience, hit **Coffee And** (530-587-3123) in old Truckee. I once counted 17 coffee refills or warm-ups during a single breakfast a couple of years ago. Of course I tottered out into the sun twitching and scratching like a meth addict, so cracked-out I could feel my hair growing. While abundant, the coffee's horrendous, so **Wild Cherries** (530-582-5602) is the only way to go for a snoot full of caffeine, baked goods and decent lunches too. Anyplace with a parking lot full of beat up trucks and a steady stream of Carhartt-wearing construction workers has to be serving high-test café two thumbs up. For Mexican food, my vote goes to **El Toro Bravo** (530-587-3557) and their outdoor patio in the summer. If you like high volume mariachi music, you're golden.

The best vibe in town award (and incredible food too) goes to **Earthly Delights** (530-587-7793) right next door to the secondhand gear shop, which stocks a good selection of used gear, and can be the ticket for a half hour mission, browsing for stuff you didn't know you needed until you saw it. If you've got a little money rattling around (uh huh, right) check out **Dragonfly** (530-587-0557), upstairs in Old Truckee. A couple of the guys that work there are super stoked on bouldering, so tip big! For a cooling libation after a hot day in the sun, my vote goes to **Bar of America** (530-587-3110) a classic dive that won't cost an arm and a leg.

North Lake Tahoe Pay Camping

Donner Memorial California State Park
Interstate 80, Truckee, CA (530) 582-7894
www.parks.ca.gov/default.asp?page_id=503

For many other pay campsites, visit: http://www.fs.fed.us/r5/tahoe/recreation/tkrd/summer.shtml or call (530) 478-6118

Winter Bouldering Areas

Bouldering in winter!? Well, if you don't mind hiking through a little snow, winter bouldering is great. The snow takes the bite off many of the highballs and is not a big deal if you bring a tarp. The following areas are climbable after 3-5 days of sun and above freezing temperatures.

North of Reno Areas
Purgatory
Washoe boulders
Hangman's Cave
Momma Cat Boulder
Sugarloaf
Echo View Estates
Pie Shop
Memorial Boulder
Rainbow
Sun Wall

Clair Tappan Lodge

This Sierra Club lodge is about 1.5 miles west of summit on Old 40 and offers innexpensive bunks and meals with a great history. Ansel Adams used to stay there and many of the old Sierra Clubbers who stared climbing in the West. The Sierra Club also owns the Hutchinson Lodge right next door. It is rented to groups at reasonable rates and is great for climbers.

Groceries

There are major supermarkets in all larger Tahoe towns. If you're staying at Lover's Leap, **Strawberry Market**, located across from Strawberry Lodge, has a selection of good essential items. You can also buy extra copies of this guide there.

South Lake Climbing Gear

The best selection of gear and climbing beta in South Lake is at **Sports Ltd.** (530) 544-2284) in South Lake Tahoe at the South Y Shopping Center next to Raley's.

North Lake Climbing Gear and Gym

There are four stores in North Lake Tahoe: **Alpenglow** (530) 583-6917 in Tahoe City, **The Backcountry** (888) 625-8444 in Tahoe City and Truckee**, Granite Chief** (530) 587-2809 in Truckee, and **The Sports Exchange** (530) 582-4510 in Truckee. The Sports Exchange also offers shoe rental ($3) and has a cool bouldering gym ($8 day pass).

South Lake Rest Days

If you need a rest day or just want to mix things up, consider riding two world-class mountain bike trails: **The Flume Trail** and **Mister Toad's Wild Ride**. In summer, buy a lift ticket to ride at a ski resort. Hike one of the many trails or head for the water of Lake Tahoe to kayak, water ski, or just sit on the beach.

For gear and recommendations from knowledgeable locals, visit **Sports Ltd.** in South Lake Tahoe at the South Y Shopping Center next to Raley's; (530) 544-2284.

Most of the nightlife is at the Harrah's or Harvey's casinos. We prefer chilling at **Divided Sky**. In the winter, take the rare opportunity to spend half the day bouldering and a half day getting powder turns at a nearby ski resort.

North Lake Rest Days

There really isn't that much to do here in the urban sense. Days off can be a bit dull if you're into city life. If not, there's a ton of good mountain biking and hiking available, plus boating and swimming at Donner Lake. Early season you can still get tracks on north facing slopes, and have a mini-adventure race: hike and then ski or board one of the peaks park at Donner Ski Ranch and bike to the Saddle Boulders, then bomb the downhill into Truckee, eat lunch and hitch or car-shuttle back up the pass. A decent rest-day excursion is driving Highway 50 to Highway 49 over to Nevada City and just hanging out. This town has a sweet, laid-back feel and makes it easy to spend a day doing nothing at all without getting bored. On the way there, take a side trip north to the town of Washington for a trip back in time. It's tiny, almost at the end of the road, and blessed with a couple of amazing swimming holes just up the river from the town. That, plus no people equals a perfect rest day.

Bouldering Ratings Compared

Vermin	Y.D.S	Fontainbleau	Peak
V0-	5.9	4	
V0	5.10a/b	4+	B0 B1
V0+	5.10c/d	5	B2
V1	5.11a/b	5+	
V2	5.11b/c	6a	B3
V3	5.11c/d	6a+ 6b	B4
V4	5.12a/b	6b+	B5
V5	5.12b/c	6c 6c+	B6
V6	5.12c/d	7a	B7
V7	5.13a/b	7a+	B8
V8	5.13b/c	7b	
V9	5.13c/d	7b+	B9
V10	5.14a	7c	B10
V11	5.14b	7c+ 8a	B11
V12	5.14c	8a+	B12
V13	5.14d	8b	B13
V14	5.15a	8b+ 8c	B14

Minimizing Impacts

Most Tahoe bouldering areas are on National Forest land and are subject to few restrictions. Let's keep it that way. Fewer environmental impacts and fewer confrontations with rangers and private landowners mean fewer restrictions on our climbing.

The Leave No Trace principles are a good place to start:

• Plan Ahead and Prepare
• Travel and Camp on Durable Surfaces
• Dispose of Waste Properly
• Leave What You Find
• Minimize Campfire Impacts
• Respect Wildlife
• Be Considerate of Other Visitors

If we all abide by these principles, we will be in good shape. But, to really preserve our climbing freedoms, we need to go beyond. The following is a list of things to do and how to get involved:

Be conscious of where you walk, where you park, and where your bouldering pad is
Most bouldering impacts come not from actually climbing, but from cutting trails to the rock and crushing vegetation with your crash pad. Always look for established trails and avoid making new shortcuts. Park in designated areas on the maps in this book. Try to carpool to areas that are accessed from residential neighborhoods. Would you want eight cars constantly parked in front of your house? If you are bouldering in the winter, make sure you are not in a snow removal zone.

Organize trail projects to reduce erosion
Trail projects come up every few years at Lover's Leap and can generally use your help. Talk to locals and find out if there is an upcoming project. You can make a difference.

Join the Access Fund
This is a terrific organization that keeps climbing areas open. In the past the Access Fund has invested its resources in preserving the Tahoe climbing experience and we should invest in them: www.accessfund.org

Don't Chip or Glue
Please don't manufacture holds (i.e. drilling and chipping). Gluing is questionable at best. There plenty of problems that go without chipping and we need to leave stuff for the future V20 climbers.

SuperTopo Mission

- Provide the resources and inspiration for an incredible outdoor adventure.

- Help climbers ascend and descend routes efficiently and safely by creating the most accurate and informative climbing topos ever published.

- Capture the mystery, adventure, and humor of climbing by publishing the histories, anecdotes, and outrageous stories of each route.

- Stress the importance of low impact climbing and promote stewardship of the environment.

- Pay close attention to your feedback to continually improve the topos and beta.

Visit www.SuperTopo.com Before Each Climb

There is much more beta available for free on the SuperTopo web site: www.supertopo.com. This information is more current than the beta available here.

SuperTopo offers additional free beta for each climb:

- photo galleries
- trip reports
- route condition updates
- closures and rockfall warnings
- route beta email alerts

The web site is packed with general Lake Tahoe info:

- free downloadable color topos
- road and weather conditions
- everything you need to know about staying in Tahoe
- good routes for first-time Tahoe climbers
- general trip planning info

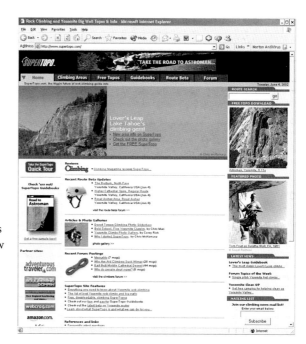

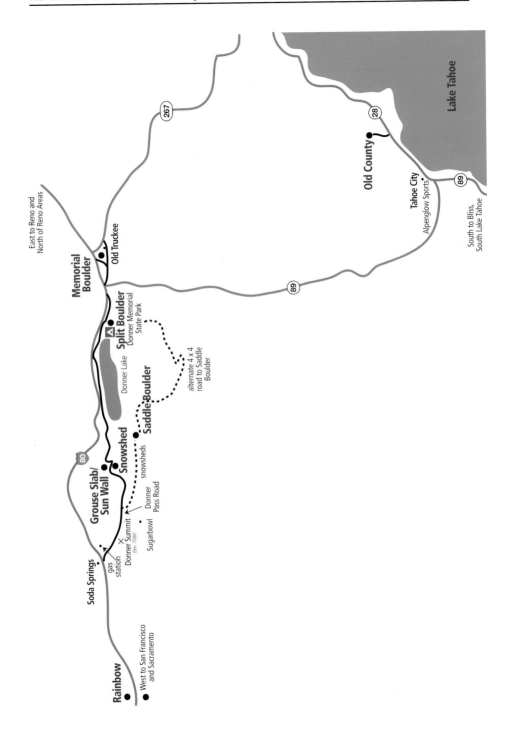

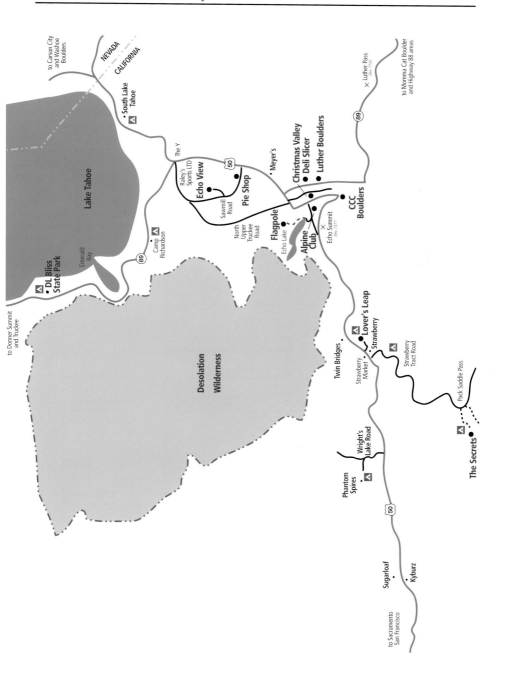

Sugarloaf

Approach time: **5-10 minutes**

Season: **Year-round**

Number of problems **10–20'**

In 2004, a fire raced up the hillside around Sugarloaf and roasted the forest. In the aftermath, many boulders that had been hidden in dense brush emerged, and a new bouldering area appeared. I say new tentatively, because some these boulders are close to the Sugarbun and may have seen some activity in the past. If they did, it wasn't much, and no evidence remained when Scott Perry started developing the place almost single-handedly. Now there are nearly sixty problems found, and only a fraction have been cleaned and climbed. This is a great place to boulder in the winter.

Some of the best are:
- Snowcat: rising V4 with a dyno
- Husky: perfect, overhanging, splitter thin-hands to fat fist crack V2
- The Wave: covered with problems, some of which are probably V7 or harder

- The Border Boulders, with a testpiece thin crack that has repelled all boarders for a year now, a contortionist problem leading into a groove, plus three other worthy problems.

Driving Directions

Sugarloaf sits above Highway 50 between Kyburz and Silverfork. From the west (Placerville), drive .4 miles past the gas station in Silver Fork and park on the right (south) side of the road in a dirt pullout across from a phone company building. From the east (South Lake Tahoe), drive 0.6 miles past Kyburz and park in the dirt pullout on the left (south) side of the road across from a phone company building. Follow a climbers' trail up and right, through a split boulder, then cut up and left. (It's more direct to hike a dirt road just west of the phone company building but this is private property). From here, the trail merges into an old 4WD road and goes straight uphill for 100 yards before turning back to a trail. See the overview map to locate each climb and formation.

Approach

The boulders are in a band that runs parallel to the Pony Express trail (marked with pink ribbons) within five minutes either side of the trail. The entire area is about a fifteen minutes walk long, from the Border Boulders to the Snowcat boulder, and almost everything is within sight of the trail. Being a new area, there's plenty of room for development and the topo is kind of vague. You'll still be able to find everything, but it won't be the Happy Boulders (thank God). Trust me, it's worth it. Get after it!

Scott Perry on The Wave.
Photo by Kevin Swift

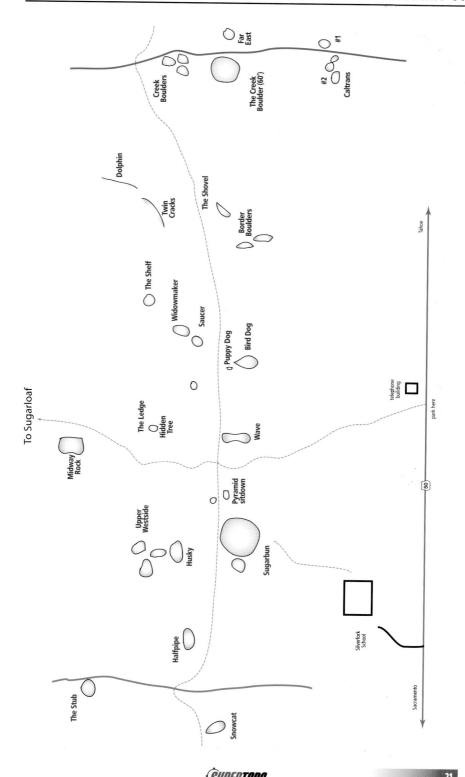

Lover's Leap Campground

Approach time: **1 minute**

Season: **April-November**

Number of problems: **50**

Mark Nicholas on Monks Rock.

Known mainly as the best moderate multi-pitch climbing in California, Lover's Leap also has a small concentration of exceptional boulder problems. The high quality granite is extremely textured and offers a wide variety of hand holds. Most problems are in the V1-V5 range and offer everything from steep crimps and slopers to long traverses and short cracks. There are enough problems for a full day of bouldering.

If it's scorching out, the river offers some great swimming holes. Or, for cooler temps, drive 15 minutes to The Secrets. Or just blow the whole day off, slackline the campground and knock back a few cold ones.

Driving Directions

From Highway 50, pull into the east end of the Strawberry Lodge parking lot. The road bends left, continues another 500 feet to a bridge that crosses the American River. Immediately after the bridge, turn left and continue up a narrow road to the campground. If the campground parking is full, park west of the Strawberry Lodge in a large pullout on the side of Highway 50. Never park in front of houses between Highway 50 and the Lover's Leap campground.

Approach

Walk east of the campground on any of the trails. After 200 feet you will see the boulders.

Number of problems by difficulty

VB	V0	V1	V2	V3	V4	V5	V6	V7	V8	V9	V10	≥V11
2	6	5	4	12	6	5	3	1	2	0	0	0

SUPERTOPO

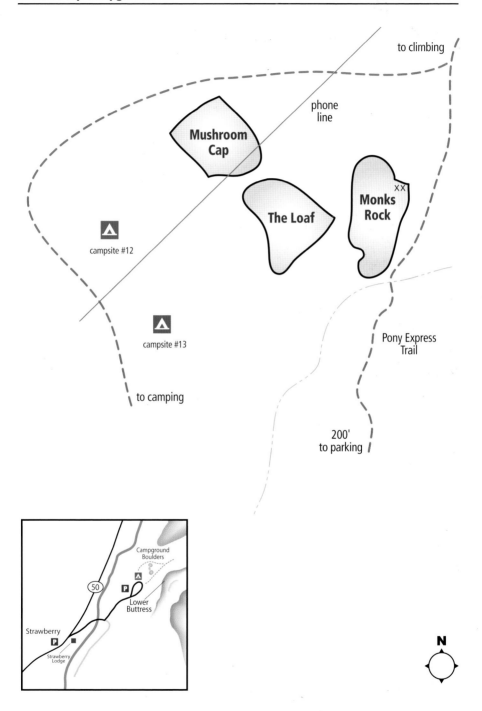

Monks Rock, Northeast Face (cave)

☐ **1. Monks Traverse V4** This 40-foot endurance test requires two or more spotters and many pads. Start by hanging on the jug at the southeast corner of the overhang. Dyno with the right hand for a crimp, then bring the feet onto the slab. Easy traverse under the roof leads to the start of Problem 3. Do initial awkward jams on 3, but instead of finishing straight up, make a pumpy traverse right on giant holds with poor feet. Turn the corner and finish by traversing the (easier) northwest face.

☐ **2. V2** This can be climbed as a boulder problem with a poor landing, or a toprope from two-bolt anchor (accessed by Problem 11). Start with thin hand jams, make a powerful and awkward move to a jug, then grunt over the bulge. Traverse left under a roof on awkward but easier moves.

☐ **3. Bachar Problem V5** Climb this as a boulder problem with a terrible, ankle-breaking landing, or a fun toprope (access anchor via Problem 11). Start on 2 but move right then straight up after pulling the first roof. The crux holds are not as positive as you would like.

Monks Rock, West Face

☐ **4. V3** A sit start then powerful moves up a short steep section join up with the large

shelf. Traverse right and finish on Problem 9 for a more difficult finish.

☐ **5. Lord of the Rings V1** Fun traverse of northwest face across wild, colored rock, then turn the corner (need a good spotter).

Robbins' Aid Ladder (not shown) – Rivets and bolts up the middle of the face.

Monks Rock, South Face

❏ **6. V0** Chimney or stem up wide crack to top of boulder.

❏ **7. V3** Powerful slapping up the arête. Optional V8 undercling start.

❏ **8. V?** Project. Horrendous slopers on a vertical wall.

❏ **9. V3** Sit start to awkward arête-wrestling, then a tough mantel.

❏ **10. V1** Pockets to sidepull.

❏ **11. VB** This arête offers the easiest access to the top. From here, you can set a toprope off a two-bolt anchor for Problems 2 and 3.

Monks Rock, North Face (not shown)

❏ **12. V1** Left crack. Overhanging and awkward hands, fist and lieback to high, but easy face finish.

❏ **13. V0** Right crack. Overhanging bomber hand jams to high but easy face finish.

❏ **14. V5** Just right of right crack. Sloper and knobs. V6 start if you traverse in from right.

The Loaf, Northeast Face

❏ **15. V3** An endurance test. Sit start backstepping right foot, then powerful move into a long hand traverse across the entire northeast face. Finish when you feel like it.

❏ **16. V0** Hand jam to mantel.

❏ **17. V0** Lieback or fist jam.

❏ **18. V3** Awkward lieback move to top.

❏ **19. V3** Sit start to two-move wonder; awkward pinch or fingerlock followed by powerful pull to jug.

❏ **20. 5.12** SDS. Hard offwidth sit start. Do this and be worshipped.

❏ **21. V3** Stand start. The easy way around the offwidth.

The Loaf, Southwest Face (not shown)

❏ **22.** **V4** Start in wide crack then head out.

❏ **23.** **V3** Gold speckle pinches.

❏ **24.** **V4** Prow sit start. Top out left side.

Mushroom Cap, Northeast Face

❏ **25.** **V2** Double dikes. Desperate slab moves up black rock.

❏ **26.** **V4** Undercling, then more desperate slab moves up rock.

❏ **27.** **V5** Good starting hold and tiny feet to thin and tricky moves to slab finish.

❏ **28.** **V6** Thin and desperate to top.

❏ **29.** **V4** Tricky traverse moves into Problem 31.

❏ **30.** **V5** Variation. A hard starting move into Problem 31.

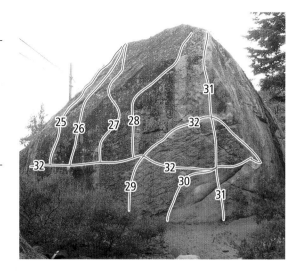

❏ **31. Paul's Problem** **V3** The most classic problem on the face. A tough start leads to a jug and then the business: grab slopers, get your feet up, and reach high. The finish is scary but manageable. Use many crash pads.

❏ **32. Boo Boos Traverse** **V6/V8** Traverse entire Northeast Face. V6 if you do once. V8 if you do the traverse and reverse. Finish on Problem 25.

Mushroom Cap, Northeast Face (left)

❏ **33.** **V1** Pinch dikes and slap arête. Awkward finish.

❏ **34.** **V0** Start on horizontal crack, then up dike to diagonal tips crack.

Mushroom Cap, Inside (not shown)

❏ **35. Birth Canal** **5.10** Squeeze chimney. Start halfway between phone pole and the north side of boulder.

❏ **36. Lightning Bolt Crack** **VB** On west-facing side of rock. Great for kids.

❏ **37.** **V8** Super hard and technical face on east-facing wall. Start seven feet north of phone pole, just right of green lichen.

❑ **38.** V4 Start left hand in crack on lichen on east-facing wall. Move up and left.

❑ **40.** V3 Just right of phone pole on east-facing wall. Height dependent.

Mushroom Cap, Northeast Face (right)

All of these problems can be toproped by building an anchor with cams and stoppers.

❑ **41.** V1 Thin locks and side pulls with mediocre feet.

❑ **42. Thin Line** V7 Really hard and technical face.

❑ **43.** V1 Powerful sidepulls.

Mushroom Cap, Southwest Face

❑ **44. Footloose** V6 Traverse entire face.

❑ **45.** V2 Start just right of arête and use crack and the many facehold options.

❑ **46. Ankle Anguish** V5 Classic. Start on crimp for hand and micro edges for feet. Go left on crack, then straight up arête.

❑ **47.** V3 Hard start to large sloper. Good fingerlock (bad feet), then big reach right. High finish on large incut holds.

❑ **48.** V3 Start in the right diagonal crack, then head straight up. Big reaches with small feet.

❑ **49.** V2 Hand traverse right then left.

❑ **50.** V5 Slopey face hold start. Big move to gain this crack.

More...

The Whale boulder has some slabs and a wild roof on the approach to the East Wall. There are also a number of problems in a cave under Tombstone Ledge.

The Secrets

Approach time: **1-5 minutes**

Season: **June-November**

Number of Problems: **200+**

There's a little slice of nirvana just three hours from the Bay Area, and 20 minutes out of Tahoe. Wherever you're coming from, be prepared for life to slow down a little when you get here. It's just far enough out to feel the pressure of normal life ease, but close enough to everything that there's no hassle involved in heading into Tahoe for whatever you need. It's even worth coming here for a couple days if you're from Tahoe, just to take a break from all the tourists. There won't be any at The Secrets.

Can you say "Motherlode?" This is one of the most extensive bouldering areas in Tahoe. Of the approximately 1,000 boulders, less than 100 have ever been climbed. This guidebook covers a tiny bit of the total problems. The rock is very similar to Phantom Spires with good quality granite with knobs. There is a boulder within 200 feet no matter what direction you walk.

With so many boulders, it's hard to know where to start. Focus on the concentrations, which are listed on the map on the facing page. For your first trip, spend the morning at The Mystics and the afternoon at The Sticks. All other areas listed on the map will have 20-40 quality problems. Because this area is so new, it was impossible to create a complete guide for every boulder in the area. By the time you read this, hundreds more boulders will have been found.

The Secrets was once Tahoe's most mysterious bouldering area. Rumors of the areas endless potential circulated wildly for a quarter century. Many people came, missed the main concentrations, and left disappointed. Until 2004, Mark Nicholas alone saw the areas potential. For 20 years he more or less had the area to himself, establishing over 100 problems, including

Mark Nicholas topping out Dunk and Dangle.

some V10 test pieces. In 2004, word spread and over 100 additional problems were established.

Boulder here as soon as the snow is clear from Strawberry Tract Road. There are a few north-facing turns that hold snow into June. The first major snowstorm usually covers the road in late November. October and November offer crisp temperatures, great fall colors on the trees, and ferns.

Driving to Pack Saddle Pass

On Highway 50, 0.5 miles west of Strawberry, turn south onto 42 Mile Track Road. Reset your odometer. After crossing a bridge, the road comes to a T intersection and you turn right onto Strawberry Tract Road. At 5.5 miles from Highway 50, you reach Pack Saddle Pass. The pass is unmarked but obvious because after the pass the road descends. At Pack Saddle Pass there are two dirt roads on your right (west). There may be a sign that says "Forest Service 71" between the two roads.

Both the Upper Road and Lower Road lead to much bouldering. But the Upper

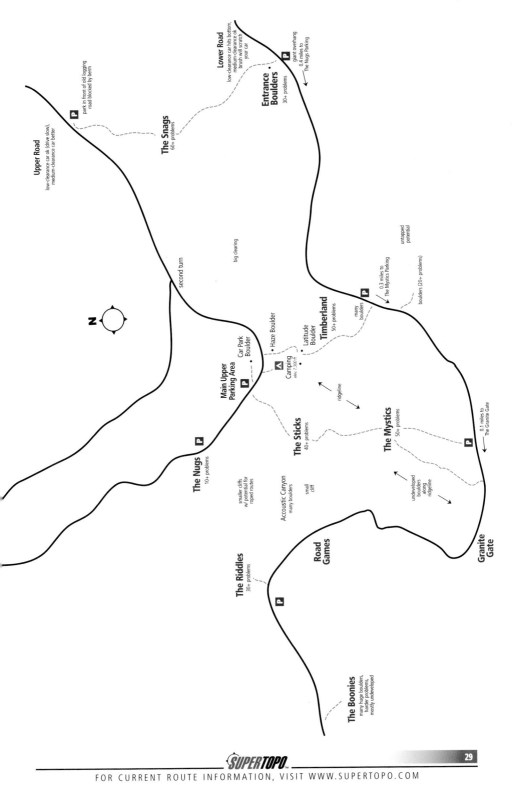

Upper Road
low-clearance car ok (drive slow),
medium-clearance car better

park in front of old logging
road blocked by berm

The Snags
60+ problems

Lower Road
low-clearance car hits bottom,
medium-clearance car ok
brush will scratch
your car

**Entrance
Boulders**
30+ problems

giant overhang
0.4 miles to
The Nugs Parking

second turn

big clearing

untapped
potential

0.3 miles to
The Mystics Parking

Timberland
50+ problems

boulders (20+ problems)

many
boulders

Haze Boulder

Latitude
Boulder

Car Park
Boulder

**Main Upper
Parking Area**

Camping
elev 7,300 ft

ridgeline

The Mystics
50+ problems

0.1 miles to
The Granite Gate

The Sticks
40+ problems

The Nugs
10+ problems

smaller cliffs
w/ potential for
roped routes

Accoustic Canyon
many boulders

small
cliff

undeveloped
boulders
along
ridgeline

The Riddles
30+ problems

**Road
Games**

**Granite
Gate**

The Boonies
many huge boulders,
harder problems,
mostly undeveloped

N

(north-most) dirt road leads to the highest concentration of established problems and is the easiest for low-clearance cars.

Driving Directions for Upper Road

From Pack Saddle Pass, take the first (north-most) dirt road. Reset your odometer. Drive about 0.7 miles and make a left on a dirt road marked by a subtle wooden post that says "10N03Y." After 0.4 miles, you reach The Snags parking (dirt pullout on left in front of a berm). Drive another 0.2 miles and stay left when the road forks. Drive 0.2 miles and park in the big pullout on the right for the Main Upper Parking Area. From here you can access The Mystics, The Sticks, and The Nugs.

GPS Coordinates for Upper Road

38 45.615 120 10.663 - Pack Saddle Pass: Upper Road turnoff
38 45.916 120 11.320 – 1st turn
38 45.803 120 11.886 – Snags Parking
38 45.547 120 11.814 – 2nd turn
38 45.453 120 11.991 – Main Upper Parking

Driving Direction for Lower Road

From Pack Saddle Pass take the second (south-most) dirt road. Reset your odometer. Drive about 0.6 miles until the road forks. Stay right. Drive about another 0.4 miles and you get to the Entrance Boulders. Keep driving and there will be boulders everywhere along the road (but the main areas require a short hike uphill). Refer to the map.

GPS Coordinates for Lower Road

38 45.616 120 10.706 – Pack Saddle Pass: Lower Road turnoff
38 45.558 120 11.298 – First right turn
38 45.417 120 11.471 – Entrance Boulders parking
38 45.309 120 11.827 – Timberland parking
38 45.174 120 12.065 – Mystics parking
38 45.156 120 12.185 – Granite Gate
38 45.422 120 12.287 – Road Games
38 45.401 120 12.403 - The Boonies

Approach

For most areas, just use the map on page 27. Some areas have specific directions.

Camping

There is great undeveloped camping on the ridgeline just a few hundred feet from the Main Upper Parking Area. You get great views south as well as morning and evening sun. You have to walk a few hundred feet for the best spots. Bring your own water, pack out your trash, and bury your waste.

But wait... There's more!

Remember, we have only shown a tiny bit of the total bouldering in this area. There is a lot more in nearby areas. How do you find new problems? Drive until something catches your eye. Walk toward it. Even if it doesn't amount to much, just walk 300 feet in any other direction and you will probably find a boulder worth climbing.

If you get seriously off track you can wander for hours and leave your oil pan and muffler behind, all to no good purpose, so stick with the mapped roads at first.

The Snags

Approach time: **3-6 minutes**

Season: **June- November**

Number of problems: **50+**

This is the most concentrated area at The Secrets with over 50 problems and lots more potential. It is also the closest major area from Pack Saddle Pass. The name stems from the numerous dead snags and logs in the area. GPS coordinates: 38 45.580 120 11.954

Approach

From the parking pullout on the Upper Road, walk over a berm and follow an old faint logging road southwest for 200 yards. Just past a rock outcropping, turn left (south) and walk a few hundred feet to the boulders.

❏ **1. Up and Down** V0 Large edges and knobs gain the top.

❏ **2. Tortoise** V1 Large holds up steep face; two topouts.

❏ **3. Rigor** V1 Small knobs on top.

❏ **4. Spotless** V2 SDS off large holds under prow/overhang to knobby finish.

❏ **5. Tailbone** V0 Only obvious line.

❏ **6. Green Hornet** V5 Balancy moves up green face.

❏ **7. Kato** V1 Climb up to finger traverse.

❏ **8. Consolation Prize** V8 Left of unclimbed overhanging arête.

Clair Nicholas on Far Right.

❏ **9. Condolences** V0 Flakes to top.

❏ **10. Adrenaline** V2/3 Obvious lieback.

❏ **11. Stinger** V4 Steep. Small holds to larger holds.

❏ **12. Flash** V7 Small knobs past mossy face.

❏ **13. Finger Death** V2 Follow finger crack to blocky summit.

❏ **14. Block Party** V0 Good warmup past blocks.

❏ **15. Crap** V0 Short lieback to top.

Number of problems by difficulty

VB	V0	V1	V2	V3	V4	V5	V6	V7	V8	V9	V10	≥V11
1	11	16	7	5	4	2	0	3	2	0	0	0

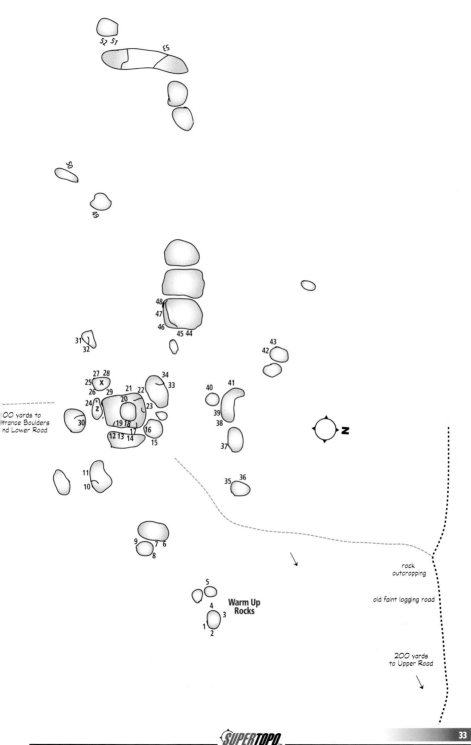

❑ **16. Mark's Marble V7** Start on small crimp or knob. Dyno to marble. Left to top.

❑ **17. Far Right V1** Obvious seam.

❑ **18. Greaser V4** Traverse on sloping edges with no feet to better edges.

❑ **19. Gobbie V4** Arête to finger crack.

❑ **20. Moss Dog V1** Lieback edge.

❑ **21. Power Extreme V7** Pull off small edges, throw into undercling with micro edge for feet.

❑ **22. Head and Shoulders V0** Right-leaning lieback.

❑ **23. Dandruff V1** Knobs to crack then right.

❑ **24. Tad's Problem V?** Chossy large holds to top.

❑ **25. Agent Orange V4** Left side of gold face. Many variations to top.

❑ **26. VACA V5** Creative eliminate. Many variations to top.

❑ **27. First Blood V1** Large holds to knobby finish.

❑ **28. Second Blood V0** Easier than 27.

❑ **29. Crud V0** Right of steep gold face.

❑ **30. Forget Me Not V1** Face climb past thin crack.

❑ **31. Mantel Man 1 V2** Dyno from large hold to sloping mantel.

❑ **32. Mantel Man 2 V3** Starts off same hold as 31. Harder mantel to top.

❑ **33. Neither Here V1** Lieback up thin edge to face holds.

❑ **34. Nor There V1** Small edges to top.

❑ **35. Vendetta V2** Turn arête from left to right.

❑ **36. Make up Your Mind V3** Traverse into tough top out left to right. Many variations.

❑ **37. Bowling Ball V1** Up obvious large hold.

❑ **38. Brontosaurus V1** Angle up and left.

❑ **39. Dyno Borg V8** From small pinch, dyno for finger knob. Right to sloper then up.

❑ **40. Go Big V0** Obvious large holds to knobs to top.

❑ **41. Elroy's Wall V0** Many variations to top.

❑ **42. Lovin' Lichen V1** Large holds up steep wall.

❑ **43. Liken Lichen V1** Use smaller holds on left.

❑ **44. Friction Addiction V0** Easy friction and small edging.

❑ **45. Cremation Traverse V3** Traverse either direction.

❑ **46. Black Widow V3** Immediately left of corner up obvious face holds. Tricky topout.

❑ **47. Anti-venom V2** Follow large holds up. Secure topout.

❑ **48. Six Feet Under V2** Start at end of 42. Move up and left.

❑ **49. Lone Ranger V2** Arête goes from both sides.

❑ **50. Tonto's Traverse V3** Traverse from right to left, avoiding top of the boulder.

❑ **51. John Doe1 V1** Finger holds to top.

❑ **52. Alias Saith V?**

❑ **53. Short Stuff VB** Obvious lieback jam.

Timberland

Approach time: **1-5 minutes**

Season: **April- November**

Number of problems: **30+**

This is the most convenient bouldering to the camping area and Main Upper Parking Area. Most of the boulders are elusive—they are hidden in the trees, a few hundred feet from each other. The Car Park Boulder and Haze Boulder are great at the end of the day when your friends start complaining of sore tips but you still want to charge. There are another 30+ boulders down at the Lower Road.

Approach

This area extends from above the Upper Road all the way to below the Lower Road. These problems are scattered everywhere. Your best bet is to follow the map.

Car Park Boulder

This boulder is located 100 feet northwest of the Main Upper Parking Area. The problems face uphill.

❏ **1. Driver's Test V1** Good warmup on obvious diagonal crack. Option SDS makes this problem a touch harder.

❏ **2. Stunt Man V4** SDS on rail to super-sized double-windmill slaps. Brute strength thuggery.

❏ **3. Parking Challenge V3** SDS then move up and right.

❏ **4. High-Rev V5** Big undercling to tricky dyno.

Number of problems by difficulty

VB	V0	V1	V2	V3	V4	V5	V6	V7	V8	V9	V10	≥V11
0	0	2	1	7	1	1	0	0	0	0	0	0

Haze Boulder

This boulder is located about 200 feet down from the road. Most of the problems face downhill.

❏ **5. Downwind** V3 Knobs to a tenuous topout.

❏ **6. Darkness at Noon** V3 SDS then straight up.

❏ **7. White Ash** V3 Underclings, sidepulls and edges up the middle of the face.

❏ **8. Air Support** V2 Undercling start right of tree.

❏ **9. Firebreak** V3 Traverse starting just right of 6 and finish on 8.

Latitudes Boulder

This boulder is near the camping area, about 100 yards from the road. There are a few futuristic problems waiting....

❏ **10. Twister** V3 Highly aesthetic diagonal crack, tenuous top-out.

❏ **11. Euphoria** V5 SDS. Move right, then back up and left.

❏ **12. High Seas** V3 Right side of the rock with slopers.

Frontier Boulder (not shown)

Close to camping. There are many VB-V1 options on the west face.

❏ **13. 40 oz. and a Mule** V3 Diagonal crack to hard knob topout.

❏ **14. Outlaw** V1 Great warmup on the west side of the boulder. Many options around it.

The Sticks

Approach time: 5 minutes

Season: June-November

Number of problems: 27+

Shane Carigan on Heads Will Roll..

The Sticks offer a high concentration of quality problems under giant lichen-covered trees. Although just minutes from the road and camping area, The Sticks have a totally secluded feel. If you link this area with The Secrets, you get an incredible circuit with over 70 problems. The area sports rock knobs, edges, and rails. Almost all the landings are flat. By the time you visit this area, there will probably be twice as many problems as listed here.

Approach

Follow the driving directions to the Upper Main Parking Area. From the downhill side of the road, pick up a climbers trail. Follow this for about 100 yards to the first problems. If you continue on the climbers trail, you will eventually pass all the problems. After the last boulder shown on the map at right, continue a few hundred yards to The Mystics.

Boulder A

Good warm-up boulder.

Scary

☐ **1. V2** Stem and lieback crack.

☐ **2. V2** SDS then up and left on rail.

Boulder B

The first stop for most boulderers.

☐ **3. V1** Face right of 4. Good warm up.

☐ **4. Heads Will Roll V4** SDS. Fun rounded knobs on distinct arête/prow.

☐ **5. V2** Gritty seamy crack with many variations.

☐ **6. Freak Show V2** Highball orange and black face.

The Sorcerer

The most concentrated boulder at The Sticks. There are at least 10 more variations around the current problems.

☐ **7. Casper V4** SDS to a few steep moves on knobs.

came close

Number of problems by difficulty

VB	V0	V1	V2	V3	V4	V5	V6	V7	V8	V9	V10	≥V11
1	0	4	9	3	6	1	2	0	0	0	0	0

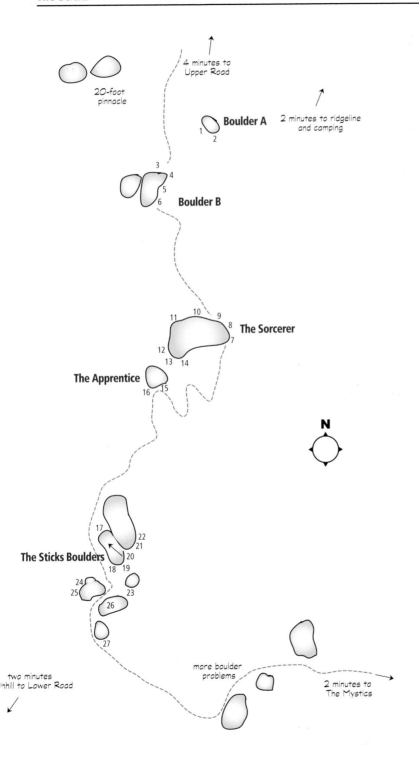

4 minutes to
Upper Road

20-foot
pinnacle

Boulder A

2 minutes to ridgeline
and camping

1
2

3
4
5
6   **Boulder B**

11   10   9
8   **The Sorcerer**
7
12
13   14

The Apprentice
15
16

N

17
22
21
The Sticks Boulders   20
18   19

24
25   23
26

27

two minutes
hill to Lower Road

more boulder
problems

2 minutes to
The Mystics

✝ ❑ **8. Thumb Buster** V2 SDS to big rounded holds.

❑ **9. The Ring** V6 Start just right of 8 and work up and right.

❑ **10. X Files** V? Project. Undercling start on black rock then diagonal up and left. Hard.

✝ ❑ **11.** V2 Several V2ish variations straight up.

✝ ❑ **12. Middle Earth** V1 Crack out of alcove.

✝ ❑ **13. Missouri Mule** V3 SDS and climb just right of crack.

❑ **14. Magic Carpet Ride** V4 Traverse that starts just right of 13 and finishes up the crack right of 10.

The Apprentice

Just down the hill from The Sorcerer.

❑ **15. Fantasia** V4 Desperate thin face moves.

❑ **16. Fear of Flying** V4 Huge windmill move. Exciting finish.

The Sticks Boulders

A cluster of boulders.

❑ **17. Pebble Wrestling** V6 Powerful knobs to easy but high finish.

❑ **18. The Sticks** V4 Pleasurable start and finish with crimpy crux in middle.

☑ **19. The Brain** V1 Mantel off big brain/ meteor.

❑ **20. Pinch** V1 SDS and climb the holds up and left with pinch finish to a reach.

☑ **21. Hound** V3 Friction feet with underclings to slopey finish.

❑ **22. Sandre the Giant** V5 SDS then up right.

South of The Sticks Boulders

❑ **23.** V2 SDS. Short but fun.

❑ **24.** V2 Avoid boulder to the left. Go straight up.

❑ **25.** V2 Up flake/seam just left of tree.

❑ **26.** VB Many easy but high problems.

❑ **27.** V3 Scary high arête.

The Mystics

Approach time: **7 minutes**

Season: **May-November**

Number of problems: **51**

This area offers the best climbing at
The Secrets. It also features the highest
concentration of problems and most varied
rock with arêtes, steep faces, traverses,
bulges, and knobs.

My first attempts at finding this place
had me convinced it was all just a vicious
sandbag by some locals with a mean sense
of humor. I drove all over and only found a
few boulders that looked decent, and many
of them needed extensive cleaning. Then
Mark Nicholas took Chris Mac out for a
tour, and when next I showed up everything
was different. There were boulders
everywhere! There's nothing like a fresh pair
of eyes to render the world comprehensible.

Approach

The approach is slightly faster if you park on
the Lower Road. However, we recommend
parking the Upper Road and then climb
at The Sticks before or after visiting The
Mystics.

From the Lower Road, hike up an old
(barely discernible) logging road. There may
be a good trail. If not, just try to stay near
the top of the ridgeline until you find the
area.

Mark Nicholas topping out Dunk and Dangle (V10)
Photo by Chris McNamara

Number of problems by difficulty

VB	V0	V1	V2	V3	V4	V5	V6	V7	V8	V9	V10	≥V11
3	8	7	7	7	6	5	2	2	2	0	2	0

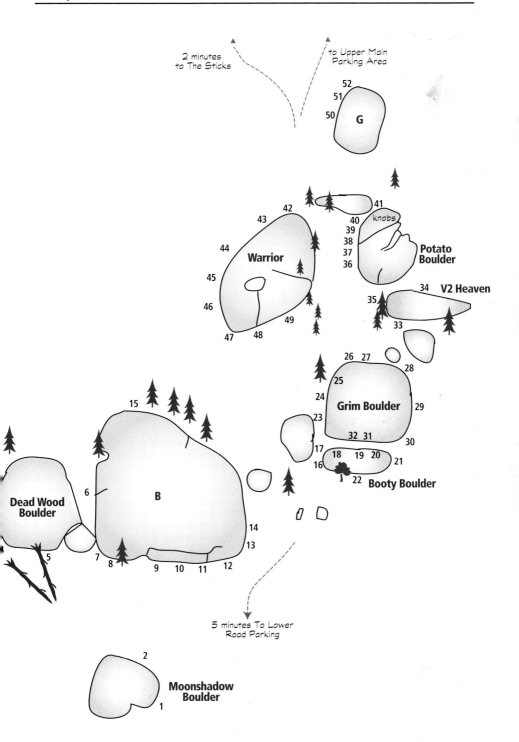

2 minutes
to The Sticks

to Upper Main
Parking Area

52
51
50
G

42
43
41
40
39
knobs
38
Warrior
37
36
Potato Boulder

44
45
46
34
V2 Heaven
35
33
47 48 49

26 27
28
25
24
Grim Boulder
23
29
32 31
30
15
17
18 19 20
16
21
22
Booty Boulder

Dead Wood Boulder
6
B
14
13
5
7
8
9 10 11 12

5 minutes To Lower
Road Parking

2
Moonshadow Boulder
1

Moonshadow Boulder

❏ **1. Moonshadow V5** Start on good hueco sidepull, climb the bulge to good edges and top out with bad holds.

❏ **2. VB** A few VB variations.

Dead Wood Boulder

❏ **3. Afterthought V3** Slopers over slightly awkward bulge.

❏ **4. Baby Bulge VB** FC.

❏ **5. Just Missed V1** Edges, undercling, and subtle footwork.

Boulder C

❏ **6. Nut Mix V4** Up and left on diagonal crack. Top out on jugs.

❏ **7. Smokin' Jacket V1** Fun problem. Two finishes. ☜ Bad Landing

❏ **8. That's Just Wrong V5** Black streak left of tree. Awkward face holds to sequential topout.

❏ **9. V2** Start with the left hand in top of seam and right hand on unique knob under roof. Go up.

❏ **10. V3** Hands on good edges. Up to knob.

❏ **11. V2** Start just right of right side of crack, then climb up and right.

❏ **12. V0** Start with right hand on big knob and left on diagonal crack. Go up on knobs.

❏ **13. V4** SDS. Powerful moves on knobs over bulge.

❏ **14. Moss Dog Traverse V3** Start as far left as you can and climb to the right.

❏ **15. Flesh Wound V4** Dyno from big flake to good ledge, then topout.

Booty Boulder

This skinny boulder is on the road side of the corridor, and has many knobs. Don't miss the arête problem.

❏ **16. It's Awl Dat V5** SDS at small knobs to the right of the crack and work your way up the arête. The stand start is more like V4.

❏ **17. Inside Voices V3** Start at the large knob at head height left of the crack and pull up into a sweet rounded topout.

❏ **18. Kinda Freaky V1** Small face holds to diagonal rail up and left. Finish finger crack.

19. Keepin' It Real V3 Thin face moves to finger crack.

20. Take the Hit V2 Low angle arête at the end of the corridor.

21. A Good Run V0 Fun arête. Easiest way to get up and down boulder.

22. Oak Tree in My Way Traverse V8 Start on the far east side of the boulder. Traverse clockwise all the way to finish on Problem 8.

Grim Boulder

23. Grim V10 Aptly named, this brutal problem is completely ridiculous. SDS. Muscle through barn door lieback to ripper finger lock. Up and right to grim finger pocket. Dyno to the top.

24. Dunk and Dangle V10 Your regular NBA problem. SDS to painful finger lock in horizontal. Get into a big undercling and dyno for a giant hold that's just a little too far away. Better do your 8 Minute Abs. The dyno alone is V7.

25. That Crack Thang V3 Hard start behind tree to easier moves along a crack. Options to finish.

26. That Knob Thing V2 Knobs at the end of a seam just left of the small tree.

27. Avoid Me V8 Tiny knobs for your left hand, nothin' much for the right, make one move up just right of the small rock hugging the wall.

28. Ghastly V0 Big knobs below a horizontal. Good fun.

29. Grisly V0 Lowangle problem at the seam.

30. Gruesome V0 Left-trending crack.

31. Gloomy V1 Slab in the corridor.

32. Glum V1 Another slab, also in the corridor.

V2 Heaven

Many V1-V2 problems/variations.

33. Celestial V2 At least four options that are all classsic V1-V2.

34. Pearly Gates V2 More classsic V1-V2 problems.

35. Golden Road V3 Cool orange plates left of tree.

Potato Boulder

Many knob problems.

36. Au Gratin V0 Just right of crack. Large knobs to right of arête.

37. Spud V0 Large knobs to shelf. Knobs to top.

38. Hash Browns V4 Go up the smallest holds to small pebbles on right.

39. Potato Head V1 Use the biggest grips to gain the summit.

40. Tater Tots V6 From SDS using finger pocket. Use the smallest hold variation up and left.

41. Ketchup V6 Athletic lieback to marble-sized knob to slopers to top.

Warrior Boulder

☐ **42. Hero Pose** V1-V2 Short problem. Overhanging slopers. Some variations.

☐ **43.** V? Project. SDS on small pinch to huge move.

☐ **44.** V? Stunning project. Bad landing. Big starting hold to slopers at lip. Dicey finish up seam.

☐ **45. Grounded** V5 Flake to right finger pocket. Swing up and right to slopers.

☐ **46.** V2-V4 Several variations on knobs and slopers.

☐ **47. Art of War** V4 Off small slopers, reach quick to gaston.

☐ **48. Crazy Horse** VB Dirty hand and lieback crack.

☐ **49. Trojan** V0 Multiple ways up slab.

Boulder G

☐ **50. Hand to Hand Combat** V4 SDS to handjam, to horizontal to more jams up and right.

☐ **51. Clandestino** V7 SDS. Up to a good left hand sidepull, then slap the slope and finish.

☐ **52. G-Ride** V7 SDS to bad slopers.

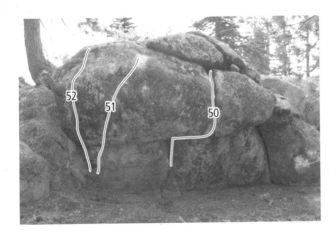

Mark Nicholas on Oak Tree in My Way Traverse (V8)

Pony Express

Approach time: **10 minutes**

Season: **June-November**

Number of problems: **15+**

Jay Sell on a fun V1 arête.

This area is more about the location and potential than the actual climbing. After a short hike on a good trail, you get to a relatively remote location. There are about 10-15 boulders in the main concentration and many more problems scattered around. The problems are mostly V0-V3 with many harder projects yet to be established. Supposedly, the true motherlode is in Sierra at Tahoe's bowl. You'll have to ask around or do some exploring yourself to find out whether the rumors are true.

Driving Directions

From Highway 50, turn south onto the Sierra At Tahoe Rd. Drive 0.9 miles and park on a small dirt shoulder on the right where the Pony Express Trail crosses the road. The trail may be hard to see. It is marked by a small plastic post with the letters XP.

Approach

Walk east on the trail. After a few hundred feet the trail turns to an old dirt road. Walk gently uphill for five minutes. The trail eventually flattens out and the tree cover thins. There is an open meadow-like area on the left and small rock outcroppings on the right that are on a broad, barely perceptible ridgeline. Leave the trail here and walk south up the slope with the rock outcroppings. Stay as high on the ridge as possible. After a few hundred yards you will come across the first boulders taller than 10 feet. This area has the most bouldering, but if you continue on the ridge and the drainage to the left, you will come across problems scattered about. GPS coordinate of boulder shown in the photo above: 38 48.548 120 04.606.

Lake Audrain

Approach time: **10 minutes**

Season: **June-November**

Number of problems: **15+**

At first glance, this area should have hundred of problems. But the rock is relatively smooth and high, which means that so far there are only about 20-30 problems established. This area is best for the adventurous boulder who doesn't mind hunting around for problems, especially high problems.

Driving Directions

Park on a huge paved pullout on the south side of Highway 50 about .5 miles west of Echo Summit or 2.1 miles east of Sierra at Tahoe.

An awesome unclimbed arête.

Approach

Hike on the dirt road for about five minutes. When the road starts to go downhill, hike 100 hundred more yards, leave the road, and hike southwest toward the ridgeline. All the boulders are on or just north of this ridgeline.

GPS Coordinates

Point where you leave the dirt road: 38 49.328 120 02.615
Location of boulders: 38 49.171 120 02.335

Bonus Area

In the same general area, there is another small boulder outcropping that has a few classic crack problems (and one really hard-looking highball arête). From the road, walk about four minutes right to where the trail starts to dip. Find the small trail on your left marked by a plastic post with the letters "XP." Follow this trail for a few minutes until you walk under the boulders.

Alpine Club

Approach time: **10 seconds**

Season: **May- November**

Number of problems: **32**

Got the barn door blues? Come here and hone your frog-sitting, swing-fighting, foot-swapping arête skills to perfection. These 12 boulders just minutes off Highway 50 provide 30 problems from VB to V7, mostly on arêtes or prows. Some of the problems lean toward highballing without quite crossing the line. If you do come off, good landings will ensure that your fingers are the only things getting sprained. These are known locally as the Berkeley Boulders, though Berkeley Camp is a mile from here, and also known as the Bower Boulders. This is one of the better mid-summer areas, as Echo Pass often has cooler temperatures than the basin.

Darrell Gschwendtner on Problem 8's splitter finger crack.

Driving Directions

On Highway 50 from Tahoe, zero your odometer at the junction with Highway 89 and go up the pass 3.2 miles to the first road on the right. Follow it through switchbacks to the Echo Summit Lodge of the California Alpine Club. Once past the lodge, drive 0.1 miles to the first left. Drive the dirt road under phone lines for a few hundred feet to the boulders.

On Highway 50 from Sacramento, zero your odometer at the Sierra at Tahoe sign on your right. At 1.7 miles, you'll see a sign for Berkeley Camp, Echo Lake, and a turn lane. Turn left here and follow this road to 2.4 miles on your odometer, then slow down to look for the entrance on your right.

You'll see a sign for 1104, Echo Summit Road, Section 5 & 6. Follow this road into the bouldering area and find limited parking along the way. The area's on your left. Please don't park in people's driveways or climb on the boulders behind the main area–they're in the residents front yards. This area could easily be gated off if summer homeowners get annoyed.

Approach

Walk 50 feet from your car to the boulders.

Number of problems by difficulty

VB	V0	V1	V2	V3	V4	V5	V6	V7	V8	V9	V10	≥V11
6	2	1	9	5	3	4	1	0	0	0	0	0

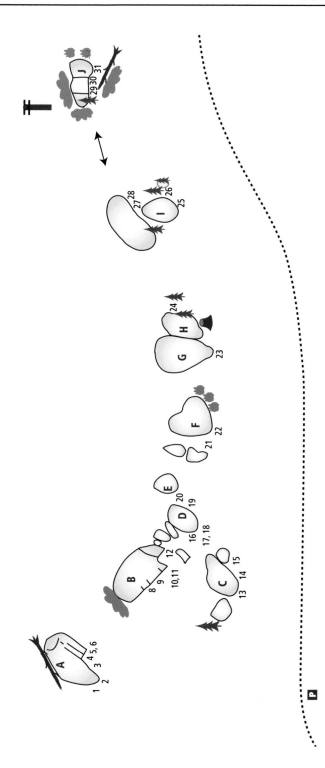

Boulder A

❏ **1. V2** Airy, slopey, and committing. Left side of the obvious, clean arête. It's slabby and a little insecure.

❏ **2. V2** The right side of the arête is good, and footwork intensive.

❏ **3. Mike Reeve's Route V5** The smooth face right of arête with committing finish.

❏ **4. VB** Climb cracks in the corner.

❏ **5. V2** The left side of the sharp, overhanging arête—harder without using the cracks.

❏ **6. V2** Fun climbing and bad landing.

Boulder B

❏ **7. V3** The far left seam with a little tree in the drop zone ends on a bad sloper.

❏ **8. V2** The thin crack just right of the seam also has an insecure, high-stepping finish.

❏ **9. V0** The right-hand crack is a good introduction to jamming skills.

❏ **10. V1** The left side of the arête, harder without the crack.

❏ **11. V2** The right side of the arête is a better problem.

❏ **12. V4** Hard start. The curved prow of the boulder just to the right of 11 has one problem on the front side.

Boulder C

❏ **13. VB** One-move mantel, on the small boulder to it's left.

❏ **14. V2** Good arête moves on slopers.

❏ **15. Another Reeve's Problem V5** This low problem requires new-wave sloping thuggery. Super cool.

Boulder D

Crimpy problems on a tall, rounded prow. All are tip-shredding fun.

❏ **16. Yabo's Gun** **V6** Fantastic. Start on the left side of the boulder on an undercling crimp. Finish with dyno on bad slopes.

❏ **17.** **V5** Different start to Yabo's Gun.

❏ **18. Been There, Done That** **V4** Starting on the right in a pocket to a series of small slopers. Feels hard.

❏ **19.** **VB** Bucket to a slab.

Boulder E

❏ **20.** **V3** Short, start on a right-facing sidepull and slap up the rounded left side.

Boulder F

❏ **21.** **V3** This hilarious, teetering high-step problem is harder if you're short and stranger if you're tall.

❏ **22.** **V5** This brutal, demoralizing SDS just right of 21 is no fun, but just frustrating and just possible enough to incite multiple tries.

Boulder G

The tallest formation here also has the best problem, a must-do that gives full value.

❏ **23.** **V4** Classic. Start at the base of the arête on the right side and swap sides, feet and hands until you topout. The face to the left of the arête might have something hard and weird, but there are some broken holds.

Boulder H

The smallish boulder right of G with two stumps in front of it.

❏ **24.** **VB** Climb the mini-dihedral on the right side, and then maybe try for something short and hard starting off the top of the big stump.

Boulder I

Hiding back from the road a little bit is a boulder that overhangs on the right side, with a tree growing just right of it.

❏ **25.** **V2** A slopey slap-fest on the rounded arête facing the road. Go up and right.

❏ **26.** **V2** Start at a good edge just behind the tree for thuggish fun.

❏ **27.** **V3** The dished face in the alcove on the back side has two different starts.

❏ **28.** **V?** The boulder just right of the V2 has something futuristic lurking on the bulge.

Boulder J

The last boulder is 200 feet farther down the road, right next to a phone pole. Not as clean as the others, but the V3 is good.

❏ **29.** **VB** The left crack.

❏ **30.** **VB** The right crack.

❏ **31.** **V3** The face right of the crack, not using the crack around the corner.

❏ **32.** **V0** The thin crack around the corner, not using the holds on the face.

CCC Boulders

Approach time: **1 minute**

Season: **May-November**

Number of problems: **30+**

This is a scattered collection of boulders by the old Civil Conservation Camp, with a few established problems hiding out on good granite. It's pretty sharp here and sees little traffic. Good fun when you deadpoint a sloper for the tenth time and slide off. There are many mantel/lip problems here. You can polish a skill that's essential, but seldom practiced. Landings here tend to be less than ideal–multiple pads and spotters will be helpful. There's potential on the hillside above the talus field encountered past the first collection of boulders. By the next edition of this book, there will probably be 60+ boulder problems at this area.

Changing aspens in October.

Driving Directions

From Tahoe, zero your odometer as you pass through the inspection station on the way out of town, about .3 miles before you start up the pass. At 4.1 miles, start watching the guardrail on the left side of the road. 50 feet past where it ends, turn left. The road is narrow, unmarked and obscure, so go slow near the guardrail's end. If you get to the road maintenance station you've gone 100 yards too far.

From the Sacramento side, you'll come up Highway 50 and pass the snow park on the right side. Then you'll see the Echo Summit sign, and the road will start to drop into the Tahoe basin. On the left, you'll see the highway maintenance yard and ahead on the right the beginning of the guardrail that runs along the outside edge of the highway. Slow down at the yard, and turn right just before the beginning of the guardrail. You can see the road better from this side than from downhill, but it's still easy to miss. If you miss it, there's a road on the left just down the pass. You can turn around here.

Once you're on the road, drive past the houses until you see an old wooden watertower on the left. The parking lot's on the right. Big enough for two cars and lined with stones. Please don't park in people's driveways.

Approach

The obvious first boulder you pass on the way in has a couple of problems, and the main boulders are along the near edge of the talus field, with some problems lurking in the talus, although with sketchy landings. If you wander around out there long enough, you'll eventually run into a few good problems, all of them steep. There's a burly cave problem on edges, and two that are reminiscent of the Bachar Cracker. (GPS coordinate for this problem is 38 48 484 120 01 796). It's worth the time it takes to find them. Good luck, 007.

The Flume

Approach time: **3 minutes**

Season: **May-November**

Number of problems: **20**

Jay Sell on a classic V2 above the water pipe.

Here are a few quality boulders with exceptional views and a unique approach. You get to the boulders by walking on a three-foot diameter steel pipe. This is an ideal place if you plan to climb at Flagpole but the weather looks iffy. What the area lacks in quantity of probems it gains in quality of rock and ambiance. There is a lot of potential down the hill.

This area is northeast facing, making it ideal for warmer days. But just about anytime of the day is good.

Driving Directions

Follow the driving directions for Flagpole Peak on the next page.

Approach

Just behind the store at the parking area, locate the metal pipe. Step on top and walk a few minutes downhill until you begin to see the boulders on your right. Within the first five minutes you will see a half dozen boulders with about a dozen problems ranging from V1 to V8. After about five minutes on the pipe from Echo Lake the pipe turns more south. At this point you can leave the pipe and scramble down the hillside for a few minutes to another cluster of boulders with some great crack problems.

GPS Cooordinates

38 50.075 120 02.653: Parking lot
38 50.067 120 02.480: First boulder

Flagpole Peak

Approach time: **20 minutes**

Season: **May-November**

Number of problems: **50+**

The massive unclimbed east face of The Overlook.
Photo by Kevin Swift

This area is absolutely fantastic—boasting superb granite, amazing views, tricky cool problems, and highballs of death. Most boulders face south so they are great in cold temperatures. In the summer, climb here in the mornings and afternoons.

A local geology buff is convinced that Echo Lake was glacially carved, and in the process bulldozed all these boulders up on the ridge before melting away. It's a good thing, too, or these great chunks of fun would be 30 feet underwater. Hmmm... How many boulders do you think are hiding underwater in the Tahoe Basin alone? How about that big wall climbing just north of D. Bliss State Park? Haven't seen it? Well, it starts out in the water, and drops 1500 feet to the bottom. If global warming really gets rolling, we might have some Yosemite-scale walls appear when the lake dries up.

Driving Directions

On Highway 50 from Tahoe, zero your odometer at the junction with Highway 89 and go up the pass 3.2 miles to the only possible road on the right. Bear right on this one-lane road, and follow it through switchbacks past the Echo Summit Lodge. Once past the lodge, look for Echo Lake Road on the right, turn right and follow it to the parking lot.

On Highway 50 from Sacramento, zero your odometer at the Sierra at Tahoe sign on your right. At 1.7 miles, you'll see a sign for Berkeley Camp, Echo Lake, and a turn lane. Turn left, drive to Echo Lake Road, turn left again, and follow it to the parking lot.

Approach

Hike the Pacific Crest Trail along the north side of the lake. After ten minutes you'll pass a house with a blue roof, then a house with a covered boat dock. Head up and right toward the obvious saddle between the ridgeline and Flagpole Peak, the granite crag facing you. On the way up the slope you'll pass three great boulders, but the real goods are below the crest on the Tahoe side. You'll see it below you—The Punisher!!

Number of problems by difficulty

VB	V0	V1	V2	V3	V4	V5	V6	V7	V8	V9	V10	≥V11
0	2	2	6	3	5	2	0	1	0	0	0	0

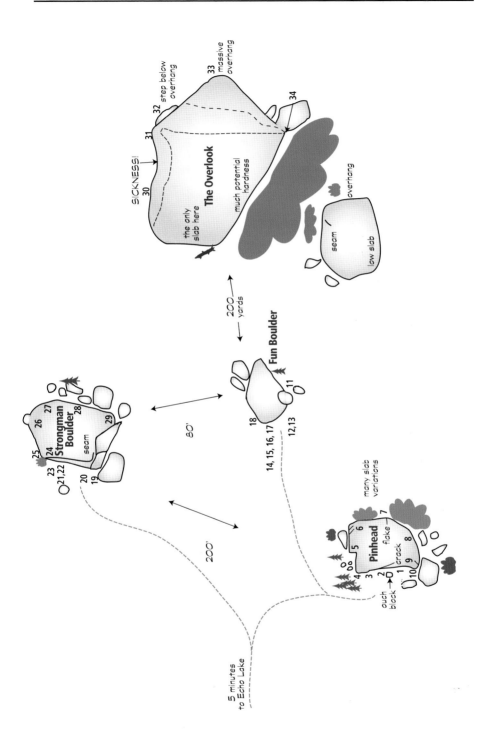

Pinhead

❏ **1. Pinhead Crack V4** Sit down, wiggle your tips into this superb thin crack and pull through the bulge. Harder than you'd think.

❏ **2. Kitty Litter V4** Well featured groove left of the crack. Start on any of a number of OK slopers, then pull up onto the slab. Harder for short folks.

❏ **3. Catfight V3** Left-trending series of flakes to a slab with a prominent gray knob. Surprisingly tenuous in spots.

❏ **4. Zippy V4** SDS. Blunt arête with a gray patch of rock by the crack.

❏ **5. Aggro Zippy V5** Scary.

❏ **6. V0** Great fun. Race along the hand traverse crack. It helps if you make monkey noises.

❏ **7. V0** Cool moves with a licheny crux. This is also the down route.

❏ **8. V1** Edges right of the seam are harder

if you start off the ground.

❏ **9. V2** Jam, lieback, and tiptoe faint seam.

❏ **10. V?** Project. This polished, round arête might go if it's cold enough.

Fun Boulder (AKA The Spud)

The Fun Boulder is aptly named, with six cool, steep problems on it, and good potential for variations.

❏ **11. V?** Start on the block and mantel the rounded, gold handrail.

❏ **12. V2** Right hand in a sidepull and left in the slot, throw to the gray edge and mantel up on the right side of the seam.

❏ **13. V4** Start where the mini-roof meets the end of the seam and dyno for the gray edge up and right.

❏ **14. V?** Project. SDS and traverse the seam from left to right.

❏ **15. White Girl V2** Grab the big, obvious edge and bounce up through the overhang on great holds.

❏ **16. Fun Girl** V7 The SDS to 15 has only had one ascent, and starts about three feet below the V1 start on bad holds by the seam.

❏ **17. Potato Eyes** V2 Same start, but traverse left around the corner on gray knobs. The tricky beta is easier than the straightforward.

❏ **18. The Peeler** V5 SDS at good patina edges and go to slopes and a dyno up and right. Subtle and satisfying for being so short.

Strongman Boulder

This boulder is on the left as you come up, and has an obvious traverse crack on the face of it. It's a project for the moment, so go tick it! The other problems are good quality, and worth doing.

❏ **19.** V? Project. Small sharp edges to sloper to right-hand end of seam. Possible SDS too.

❏ **20.** V? Project. SDS at a broken right-facing sidepull on the right side of green lichen patch and dyno to the seam, then finish as 19.

❏ **21.** V? Project. SDS at the far left side of the seam and traverse the entire face left to right.

❏ **22.** V? Project. Start at the best hold in the horizontal crack and crank up to plates. Wicked hard start.

❏ **23.** V2 Start behind the small boulder, high horizontal edges lead into scoop. Taller than it looks.

❏ **24.** V? Project. A right-facing sidepull leads you around the left-hand arête into a mini-dihedral. The SDS is harder.

❏ **25.** V3 Short jumpstart to a mantel.

❏ **26.** V1 Mantel the rail to the slab.

❏ **27.** V2 Left-facing rail leads to insecure slopes.

❏ **28. Genuine Fake** V5 Alcove start on small holds. Turn bulge.

The Overlook

This boulder is just down the far side of the saddle facing into the Tahoe basin, and remains largely undeveloped, with a ton of futuristic potential. Everything here is either hard or scary—oh joy. Approach from the right side of the Fun Boulder.

☐ **30. V4** This problem is on the left side as you approach, and is the only really obvious line on this side. Start in the horizontal crack and go up and left through great holds to a spicy finish.

☐ **31. 5.12** Toprope problems straight down from two-bolt anchor.

☐ **32. Built to Last 5.13?** Project. This seven-bolt route is still being worked.

☐ **33. V3** On the small subsidiary block

below the massive overhang that faces the airport, there's a SDS to some slopers on a left-leaning arête with a great pocket just left of the arête. Kinda tall, hard finish.

☐ **34. The Punisher V?** Project. This is the most inspiring line I've seen in Tahoe, and that's saying a lot. It's 40 feet tall, exposed, steep, and has a gory-looking mantel about 18 feet up. Come out when there's a ton of snow so you don't die when you pitch off the last moves, and wear a transceiver so your spotter can find you.

The Overlook: Massive and mostly unclimbed. Probably the raddest boulder in Tahoe. See person in bottom right corner, below The Punisher, for scale.

Deli Slicer

Approach time: **7 minutes**

Season: **April-November**

Number of problems: **19**

The area around the Deli Slicer looks like God got surly drunk one night, grabbed his 12 gauge and pumped a few rounds of buckshot into the hillside. There's so many damn boulders out here you'll never do all the problems. I don't care if you live to be a hundred. Fortunately, most of them are undeveloped and obscure, otherwise this guide would be the size of a dictionary.

I have no idea how this thing got its name. It doesn't really matter – the thing to remember is that this is good stuff. Positive edges on golden patina, a hillside location with views of Christmas Valley and a seven-minute approach. The traverse in the corridor behind the main boulder is absolutely classic and plenty hard.

The boulders face west and get afternoon sun. Climb here in the morning in warm weather and in the afternoon in winter.

Driving Directions

Turn west on Highway 89 at the north end of Meyers. The third road on your left is Cornellian—turn here, then right on Elmwood. Elmwood will dead-end. Park.

Approach

Follow the trail that starts from the dead-end. There are a bunch of other trails between here and there, so pay attention. Just after you get into the trees there's a faint trail on the left. Ignore this and continue to the next intersection. Go left here on a less-obvious trail, as the better trail straight ahead ends at a huge deadfall. You'll make a horseshoe around the deadfall, and then come to another good trail that runs up the hill to your left. It should be subtly dished, like an old streambed. Follow this trail uphill for about a minute, until you come to a group of bleached logs lying to the right of the trail. Step over them, turn right, and you're on the trail to the Slicer. Uphill and right four minutes is your objective. The trail will run into the boulders you want, the first of which has a serpentine crack that runs all the way through it. If you're bushwhacking, you're off-route. Routes are described counter-clockwise from where you first come up to the boulder.

3 minute to grainy highballs o' doom

overhung corridor **B** *steep*

D

19

16 17 18

C

15

13 14 10

11 9 8 7

12 **A** 6

1 4 5

2 3

7 minute to **P**

one big bo

Number of problems by difficulty

VB	V0	V1	V2	V3	V4	V5	V6	V7	V8	V9	V10	≥V11
1	3	1	4	1	3	1	0	0	2	0	0	0

Deli Slicer Boulder

❏ **1. V4** Start on small edges just where the trail comes up, go up and left.

❏ **2. V4** Small edges just left of the crack. Don't use the crack. Bad feet, frustrating.

❏ **3. V0** Climb the crack.

❏ **4. V2** Great patina edges lead to an insecure topout, right of the crack. Feels hard due to the finish.

❏ **5. Project** There's probably something possible here, but it will be on tiny holds.

❏ **6. V0** Start in the mini-dihedral.

❏ **7. V0** Start on the prow right of the dihedral.

❏ **8. V2** Straight up from the left-facing sidepulls – watch the exit, it's got a couple flakes that are fragile and not safe to use.

❏ **9. V2** Up the edges left of the crack.

❏ **10. VB** Lieback and jam the wide crack.

❏ **11. V2** Edges on the rounded arête right of the crack. Needs cleaning.

❏ **12. V1** Start in the bushes, follow the dirty edges up to a licheny finish.

Around the Deli

Uphill there's a cluster of boulders, several of which form a corridor. The problems below are on the well-featured overhanging face right of the corridor.

❏ **13. V8?** Fantastic. Tahoe's answer to the Martini Roof, though much easier. SDS on a left-facing edge six feet left of where the corridor starts. Traverse the entire face out and right, and finish on a difficult mantel. Have a spotter for your head. If you blow off an edge you can hit the wall behind you pretty hard.

❏ **14. V8?** Up problem to a hard, sloping topout. Dangerous landing due to the boulder underneath. Pad this well, and get somebody to watch your back.

❏ **15. V?** Start on the round, extruded feature in the center of the face, and finish slightly right, on the end of 13.

Around the Deli (cont'd)

On the shorter face in front of the corridor there are some hard, crimpy problems.

❏ **16.** V3 SDS on good edges.

❏ **17.** V4 Start just left of 16, finish up and left.

❏ **18.** V? There may be something on this long face, but it'll be damn hard.

Above the corridor there is a small, round boulder with one problem starting in a depression below it.

❏ **19.** V1 SDS with good features but too short.

There's a low face left of the round boulder that's got some sit-downs, but they're not that great and mostly just one move.

Three minutes above and left of the main area, there's a cliff band that has some potential in the form of scary highball/topropes. Also, if you go straight at the bleached logs, instead of right to the Slicer, there's another group of lower quality boulders that might yield some interest with a good scrubbing. One holds a giant right-trending highball over a scary landing that looks about V2. It'd be a good test of nerves to try for the OS, armed only with a brush and your wits.

While the Deli Slicer holds the highest concentration of good problems in the immediate vicinity, the hillside it's sitting on stretches for miles up Highway 89. There are a couple full-on climbing areas up here too, and the potential is endless. Bring your posse, bring your pads, and bring the ruckus because this area needs it.

Luther/Slutty Boulders

Approach time: **1 minute**

Season: **April-November**

Number of problems: **100+**

These two bouldering areas are conveniently located just a few hundred feet off Highway 89. Come here for a late afternoon bouldering session in colder weather or, during the summer, climb in the shade before noon. There are some safe hard problems and many easier highballs. The rock quality is similar to other Christmas Valley areas but much finer and better than the Deli Slicer.

Driving Directions

From the junction of Highway 89 and 50, drive just over three miles south on 89 and park in first paved pullout on the right for the Slutty Boulders and the second paved pullout for the Luther Boulders.

Slutty Boulders

From the middle of the first paved pullout, scramble up the road cut. After a few hundred feet you will either run into the Slutty Boulders or the wide 20-foot-tall wall that sits 200 feet to the north. The Slutty Boulders have a single boulder with some great V4-V8 problems. There are also a few V1-V3 scary highballs nearby. The wide-20-foot-wide wall will have a number of really cool highballs in the future.

Luther Boulders

From the north end of the second pullout, hike northeast to the clump of boulders. There are a number of tall crack problems and a few tall face problems. Most problems are in the V1-V4 range. There is also an amazing V7 that starts at the lip of a cave.

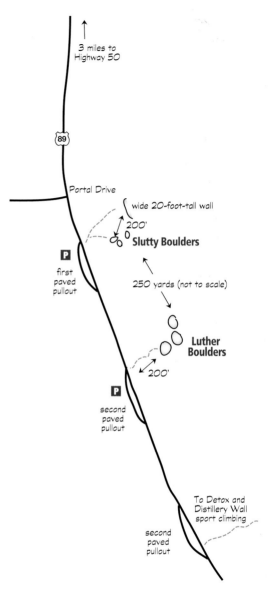

Christmas Valley

Approach time: **1-20 minutes**

Season: **March-December**

Number of problems: **50+**

Elisa Safanda on classic Tahoe granite.
Photo by David Safanda

Everybody, just chill. This is the place for a leisurely afternoon of ambling through the forest and pulling down some moderates. Good in the morning and evening, although summer brings out the mosquitoes here. There are a bunch of short boulders out here, perfect for someone who's just starting out or not yet comfortable with heights.

An interesting thing happened to me here, while checking out these boulders for the first time. I drove out and wandered around for an hour or so, trying problems as I found them and enjoying the vibe. Light gray clouds and a cool breeze made for perfect conditions. I'd had good success before coming across a crimpy, painful sit start in the middle of the area. It led to a good-sized dyno, and I was having no luck at all, getting spit off time after time. Worse, I'd gotten this stupid rap lyric stuck in my head and it kept repeating over and over, distracting me.

I was chalking up for another go when a single immense lightning bolt hit the ridgeline just a couple hundred yards away. The flash and thunder came in the same instant, as if Thor's hammer had struck sparks from the earth, and for long moments afterward the bolt's path was imprinted on my retinas. Simultaneously, the repeated lyric vanished and my thoughts stopped completely. I was snapped back into the here and now by the shock and, interestingly, the problem went down on my next attempt. It seems my newly regained presence of mind was all that had been missing on my failed attempts before.

Driving Directions

From Highway 50, turn onto South Upper Truckee road and zero your odometer. At 1.7 miles, you'll see a large pullout on the left and your first glimpse of one boulder to the right. The area starts here and runs half a mile along a bike path. The boulders are scattered within 50 yards of either side of the path and yield a few problems each that tend toward fingery sequences. The landings here are quite good, on soft pine duff. There's enough here for a short day if you have a few people along, or an evening if you're solo and motivated. Boulders are described starting from the side nearest Celio Ranch, going left.

Number of problems by difficulty

VB	V0	V1	V2	V3	V4	V5	V6	V7	V8	V9	V10	≥V11
8	9	5	11	2	6	5	3	1	0	0	0	0

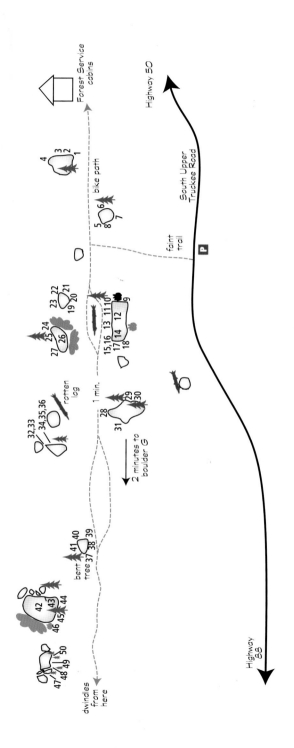

Cabin Boy

The boulder nearest the cabins doesn't offer much. It's slabby and mossy.

❏ **1. V0** Just right of tree.

❏ **2. V0** Left side of slab.

❏ **3. V1** Center of slab, small edges.

❏ **4. VB**

Manzanita Boulder

Across the path and south 200 feet is a small boulder with some short move problems.

❏ **5. VB** On the arête with the white patina.

❏ **6. V0** SDS just right of the forked tree.

❏ **7. V1** On the prow.

❏ **8. V0** SDS edges just right of arête.

❏ **.** **V0** Traverse the entire boulder starting on northwest side on obvious rounded hold. Stay in the middle of the boulder (don't grab the top).

The next boulder south is also small, and has one V0 on the arête near the trail.

The Grinch

The obvious block visible from the road across from the parking lot has a concentration of quality problems with decent landings.

❏ **9. VB** Up the blocky, mossy face.

❏ **10. V0** Through the small roof on the left side of the prow.

❏ **11. V2** Start on low, left-facing sidepull.

❏ **12. V2** Pocket and square edges, go up, then left.

❏ **13. V2** SDS dyno from the rail and incut triangle up and right to the lip.

❏ **14. V1** SDS below the triangular bulge. Go right, then back left.

❏ **15. V2** Left side of mini-dihedral, up and left.

❏ **16. V2** Same start, straight up bulging prow.

❏ **17. V5** SDS, sidepulls, bad feet.

❏ **18. V3** Rising left traverse, start on low blocky arête.

Slap Happy

Small block just north of the larger boulder described below, with five short problems.

❏ **19. Slap Happy V3** Start on low left sloper on the left side of the arête.

❏ **20. Beached V4** SDS on the right side. A frustrating four moves.

❏ **21. V1** Left side of small overhang.

❏ **22. Grinder V4** Low start, right side of overhang on small edges. Not fun, but good value.

❏ **23. VB**

Lowbrow Boulder

This boulder is hiding up the hill about 30 yards off the path. Doesn't look like much, but the back side's all right.

❏ **24. Lowbrow V5** SDS. Crimps on the rounded corner. Good.

❏ **25. V2** Low start.

❏ **26. V0** In the center of the face.

❏ **27. V6** Awkward SDS on small edges and the arête, rises to the left.

Tall Boy

This taller obelisk is a one-minute walk south from the blocky boulder nearest the parking area. The two problems between the trees are stellar.

❏ **28.** VB Slabby, rounded arête.

❏ **29.** V7 SDS just left of the big tree, straight up. V4 if you traverse into #30.

❏ **30.** V4 Start right of the small tree, rising to the right.

❏ **31.** V0 Slab right of rounded arête on small edges.

Across the path from Boulder F is a triangle boulder with some short VB's and a large, low boulder with one V2 right of the tree. Both need cleaning.

At about 5 o'clock to F, just off South Upper Truckee, there's a small block with two VB's on the north side of it.

Car Crash and Impact Boulders

A few hundred feet west of Tall Boy. The problems are listed right to left.

❏ **32. Car Crash** V5 Right boulder. Low start on horizontals with left hand on sloper. Power up over the steep prow.

❏ **33. Out of Gas** V6 SDS. Awkward sit to thin holds.

❏ **34. Pump the Brakes** V5 Right hand pumps up rounded rib.

❏ **35. Off the Edge** V5 Grab the thin knife edges.

❏ **36. Off the Slope** V2 Start both hands on rounded sloper.

High Boy

Two minutes farther along the path from Boulder F there's a rock just off the path with a bent tree growing against the left-hand arête. The problems on the left sucker you off the ground with easy starting moves, then finish with odd, unbalanced mantels.

❏ **37.** V4 Hard, sloping topout.

❏ **38. High Boy** V2 Harder if you're short, with a strange finish.

❏ **39.** V1 On prow, fun moves.

❏ **40. Unbreakabill** VB

❏ **41.** VB

Lean and Mean

❏ **42. Lean and Mean** V1 Cool, thin crack problem. Sit start is V3 or V4.

❏ **43.** V2 Strange moves into a licheny scoop. Easier than it looks.

❏ **44.** V0 Overhang.

❏ **45.** V2 SDS awkward. Traverse dirty crack.

❏ **46.** VB Slab above bushes.

Lean-To Roof

There's a small cave screened by some trees less than one minute off the path with unusual and hard-to-figure-out problems.

❏ **47. Lean-To** V6 Cool, crack problem.

❏ **48.** V4 Strange moves into a licheny scoop. Easier than it looks.

❏ **49.** V? Project. SDS into sidepulls, then dyno to the lip and finish on 50.

❏ **50. Monkey Boy** V2 Ridiculous, knee-scraping mantel. No jump-starts, and no using the tree!

Pie Shop

Approach time: **1 minute**

Season: **April-November**

Number of problems: **100**

There used to be a pie shop right near Sawmill Road, where you turn off to find these boulders. Supposedly, the pies were fantastic, but the shop's long gone. It's too bad, but change is the only thing you can depend on.

The stone here is not quite as good as Echo View, but the problems are widely varied from short and hard to moderate highballs. On a summer day Echo will torch you, so this is the ticket. Come to the forest and hang out in the shade, tick some scary stuff, and then hit the lake. Pie Shop's just ten minutes from the Y, which makes it perfect for a burn after work.

Driving Directions

Pie Shop bouldering is located in the trees just off Sawmill Road, 1.4 miles from the junction with Highway 50. Park on either side of the road in indistinct pull-outs. The boulders are on the uphill side. Straight up from the parking lot is a dense central area, with some scattered boulders higher up the hillside to the left. The layout is kind of confusing, with boulders stacked up next to and on top of each other, and what looks like the direct approach often isn't, but after one session you will have it dialed. You'll see the rocks from the road.

Kevin Swift on Razor.

Number of problems by difficulty

VB	V0	V1	V2	V3	V4	V5	V6	V7	V8	V9	V10	≥V11
7	12	6	19	23	7	2	2	3	0	0	0	0

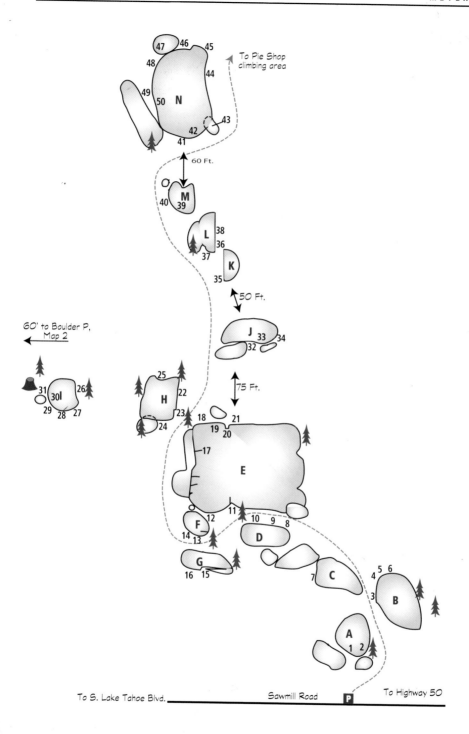

To Pie Shop climbing area

60 Ft.

50 Ft.

75 Ft.

60' to Boulder P,
Map 2

To S. Lake Tahoe Blvd.

Sawmill Road

To Highway 50

The Pig

❏ **1. The Pig** V4 Steep problem nestled between two boulders. Jug with right to big throw and precarious topout. Sickly hard futuristic SDS may not have been done. Much easier (V3) if you finish out left.

❏ **2.** V6 Super thin face ten feet right of Problem 1.

Boulder B

❏ **3.** V0 Climb orange plates on the west side of boulder.

❏ **4.** V0 Low angle arête.

❏ **5.** V1 Delicate edging and smearing five feet left of arête.

❏ **6.** V3 Obscure difficult slab on tiny holds.

Boulder C

❏ **7.** V4 One-move wonder. Left hand on broken flake, right hand on sloper. Jump.

Boulder D

❏ **8.** V2 SDS on big flake in corridor. Follow left-facing sidepull over bulge.

❏ **9.** V2 Fun liebacking up left side of detached flake.

❏ **10.** V3 Right side of same flake. Big undercling move.

Boulder E (South Side)

❏ **11.** V3 Devious seam move.

❏ **12.** V2 Precarious edges to mantel.

Boulder F

❏ **13.** V2 Start low on gray knob and crack through well-featured orange rock. Bad landing.

❏ **14.** V3 Climb rounded arête left of 13. Hard first move to odd slopers. Bad landing.

Boulder G

❏ **15. Razor** **V1** Long aesthetic razor-blade-sharp flake.

❏ **16.** **V2** Beautiful, towering, delicate highball with a catastrophic landing.

Boulder E (North Side)

❏ **17.** **V0** Grainy highball jam crack.

❏ **18. The Thing** **V8/9** Long-standing one bolt project with attempts by many big names. Mike Njoten finally led it summer of '05.

❏ **19.** **V?** Project. Tall, scary, grungy.

❏ **20.** **V2** We included this disgusting offwidth just for fun.

❏ **21.** **V4** Starts on Problem 20. Traverse the crack up and left to the first obvious break and mantel.

Boulder H

❏ **22.** **V3** SDS just right of tree at big jugs along seam. Two moves. Mantel.

❏ **23.** **V3** SDS left of tree on left-facing sidepull.

❏ **24.** **V7** Heinously thuggish. SDS with feet under cave/boulder. POWER move to the lip.

❏ **25.** **V?** Project. Lie-down start. Grovel up steep rounded seam.

Fiber Boulder (I)

❏ **26.** **V1** Tiny right facing seam/sidepull. Just off vertical.

❏ **27.** **VB** SDS at gray cobble below orange streak arête.

❏ **28.** **VB** Follow slabby right-trending crack.

❏ **29. Moving On** **V4** Good moves over bulge at converging seams.

❏ **30.** **V?** Project. Dangerous SDS. Red edge left hand. Small sidepull right hand. Have a spotter for the boulder behind you.

❏ **31.** **V?** Project. SDS at tiny seam. Looks like brutal sidepulling.

Boulder J

❑ **32. V5** Frustrating micro crystals below water streak.

❑ **33. V0** Tortoise shell patina feature directly over small boulder. Awkward.

❑ **34. V0** Low start at crumbly jugs just right of small boulder.

Boulder K

❑ **35. V?** Project. Downhill arête of distinctive split boulder. Ultra hard.

❑ **36. V4** Uphill arête. not the greatest rock quality. Balancy and strange.

Boulder L

❑ **37. V?** Project. Other half of Boulder K.

❑ **38. V?** Many slab variations are possible on low-angle right side of Boulder L.

Mars Boulder (M)

❑ **39. Mars Attacks V3** SDS at hole. Climb alien brain patina features.

❑ **40. V4** Same start as 39. Climb left of the bulge in a small groove to an awkward mantel.

Boulder N

❑ **41. V7** Reach high to start. Orange edges on black rock. Bulge to slab.

❑ **42. V3** Right hand undercling above chalk grafito. Left hand edge on face. Start off block.

❑ **43. V3** High start off of block in center of square cut roof. Edges and side pulls to mantel. Careful about the landing.

❑ **44. V?** Project. High start on pinch and sloper leads to mantel. Looks desperate.

❑ **45. V3** Great edges and slopes on bulge. Bad feet.

❑ **46. V?** Low start in cave. Right hand rail.

❑ **47. V?** SDS between Boulder N and subsidiary block. Fist to hand crack.

❑ **48. V?** Reach high and grab white bucket just right of crack. Big move to top.

❑ **49. V?** Project. Breakable flake at head height with bad feet. One desperate move to good edges.

❑ **50. V0** Two big edges above boulder.

Boulder O

This boulder sits by itself closer to the road.t

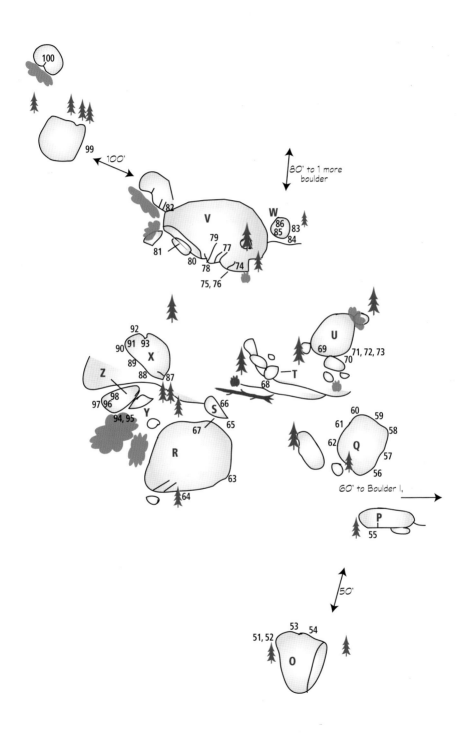

than the others.

❏ **51. V3** Traverse the horizontal crack from right to left.

❏ **52. V3** SDS, then climb into the scoop on the arête left of the tree. First move crux

❏ **53. V2** SDS A low shelf and finish liebacking the crack above.

❏ **54. V2** Same start but end on good patina left of the crack.

Boulder P

This lowangle band is level with Boulder I.

❏ **55. VB** Many scruffy variations can be found here.

Boulder Q

A small tree touches the bottom side, and good problems on the uphill side.

❏ **56. V5** A vicious opening move on clean, tiny crystals leads to mellower slabbiness above.

❏ **57. V4** This obscure problem isn't as clean, or as hard. Five feet right of 56.

❏ **58. V2** Palm the low-angle arête above a first-move crux.

❏ **59. V3** Super fun traverse on pockets to slopers. Possible traverse of this side of boulder, ending at 62.

❏ **60. V2** Straightforward crank off a right-facing sidepull leads to the middle of 59.

❏ **61. V3** Start with your left hand in the biggest drilled pocket, right hand on an edge, and go straight up.

❏ **62. V3** Skip the pockets, starting on the rounded bulge four feet right of 61.

Boulder R

Big ol' blob of stuff with nothin' much on it.

❏ **63. V?** Project. This steep, orange face has a SDS under an overhang at a seam.

❏ **64. VB** Mega-highballs everywhere, but they're bland and unspectacular.

The Orca Boulder (Boulder S)

Here's another neatly split boulder, but where's the other half?

❏ **65. V7** This steep, grainy prow has better moves than rock, but watch the sloped landing.

❏ **66. V?** Project. Tiny, fragile stuff keeps breaking, and it was speculative anyway. Good luck starting five feet left of the arête.

❏ **67. V?** Project. Godawful sloper madness on a slab opposite 66.

Boulder T

A smallish nugget perched above the long, low rock band.

❏ **68. V?** Great orange crimps, bad gray landing.

Boulder U

The next boulder uphill from Q has problems on the downhill side.

❏ **69. V0** Sweet moves along a square cut lieback above a smaller boulder. Starting without the boulder is harder.

❏ **70. V2** Height-dependent high-step move leads to orange knobs and slopers on a slab.

❏ **71. V2** Heel hook the great holds by the prow, and then beach yourself to get the good knobs in the middle of 70.

❏ **72. V2** Same start, but climb up and right along the prow.

❏ **73. V3** Start low on a gray knob two feet down and right of 72.

Boulder V

This big cliff band has a collection of low-angle highballs.

❑ **74. V1** A short slab on decent holds just left of the bush.

❑ **75. V1** Start on a slab and head up to a crack that heads right about 8 feet up.

❑ **76. V0** Start in the crack and follow it up and right.

❑ **77. VB** Head up the next crack left on easy liebacking.

❑ **78. V0** Crank up the awkward, flaring wide crack.

❑ **79. V0** Hand crack starts at a low, mini-roof with big holds. The first highball.

❑ **80. V2** Grab a good edge below a faint seam just left of 79 and pull onto the slab. First move crux.

❑ **81. V3** Start under the mini-roof and pull over the lip at a big horizontal hold. Mantel is the crux.

❑ **82. V0** Great crack moves with a tall slab finish.

Boulder W

Small boulder, big fun. These are pretty cool.

❑ **83. V3** Low start in a subtle scoop facing the tree on good edges.

❑ **84. V4** Hard SDS at two small flakes under a sharp undercling.

❑ **85. V3** Low start on a right trending seam to painful crystal crimping just left of 84.

❑ **86. V3** Low start on patina flakes, ending at a huge jug over the lip.

Boulder X

This boulder sits above the rock band that starts under Boulder S.

☐ **87. V3** Contrived SDS to short roof crack.

☐ **88. VB** Low start on cool patina flakes above a tiny tree.

☐ **89. V2** More great patina on a slab. Careful of the landing.

☐ **90. V2** Start at the obvious clean knob on the prow left of 89. Worse landing.

☐ **91. V0** Slab between the two arêtes with a boulder in the drop zone.

☐ **92. V2** Great, tall, balancy arête.

☐ **93. VB** Chimney.

Boulder Y

Triangular block just left of the three trees above Boulder R.

☐ **94. V2** SDS to a fist crack. Probably never destined to be a classic.

☐ **95. V1** Traverse the top of Y up and right from the crack.

Boulder Z

This boulder has a flat, vertical face with a finger crack facing uphill.

☐ **96. V?** Project. Jumpstart the slab to a red edge above head height.

☐ **97. V?** Project. Slopes on the low-angle rounded prow.

☐ **98. V?** Project. Desperate finger crack in chimney between Boulder Z and the rock band below Boulder X.

Boulder A1

A single problem that faces the uphill side of Boulder V.

☐ **99. V2** Good edges. Too short.

Boulder B1

The boulder up and left from A1 is pretty much the end of it.

☐ **100. V3** Height-dependent high-step to liebacking on a thin crack that splits the boulder.

Echo View

Approach time: **10 seconds**

Season: **April-November**

Number of problems: **68**

Corey Rich going for Hang Time.

Echo View is one of the best concentrated and most convenient areas in South Lake Tahoe. It sits on a sandy, wide-open hillside that faces west, overlooking Sawmill Road. The granite is abrasive, similar to that found in the Buttermilks, with occasional patches of decomposed rock. Most of the landings are decent, with occasional buried rocks that need padding.

If you're up here on an evening in the spring, when it's over don't take off right away or you'll miss the show. Instead, drag a Crazy Creek and your down jacket out on top of Boulder D, wrap your raw tips around a cold beverage and kick back for awhile. The sun will sink below the ridge line, and provide the perfect sunset backdrop to end the day. If you can sit a little longer, enjoy the evening glow as the sky runs purple into midnight blue and the black overhead opens up into stars.

Sometimes the pack of coyotes that live down the valley will serenade you with a chorus of yips and howls as they celebrate the start of another night's hunting. Later than that, which will probably require some extra layers, you can go back out for another burn under the moon and enjoy a moderate circuit all in black and white, like inhabiting an old movie.

When to climb

Spring and fall, conditions here are ideal during the day, especially in the early afternoon. A colder day will leave the granite extra sticky, and everything will feel a grade easier. In the summer when it's hot, get here early. By afternoon all the problems are cooked and won't be cool until the next morning. You can usually boulder here all winter.

Driving Directions

On Highway 50, a few miles north of Meyers, turn west onto Sawmill Road. Follow Sawmill to Echo View Drive, turn right, and head up the hill to Mt. Canary Drive. Take another right, and drive to a dead-end at a dirt parking lot with a sign reading "Twining's Stonehenge" nailed to a tree. The boulders are right in front of you. The parking lot is next to a vacation rental (which has a boulder built into one wall), and the people who own it are friendly for now. Please help keep it that way.

Number of problems by difficulty

VB	V0	V1	V2	V3	V4	V5	V6	V7	V8	V9	V10	≥V11
3	7	7	18	13	9	1	1	2	0	1	0	0

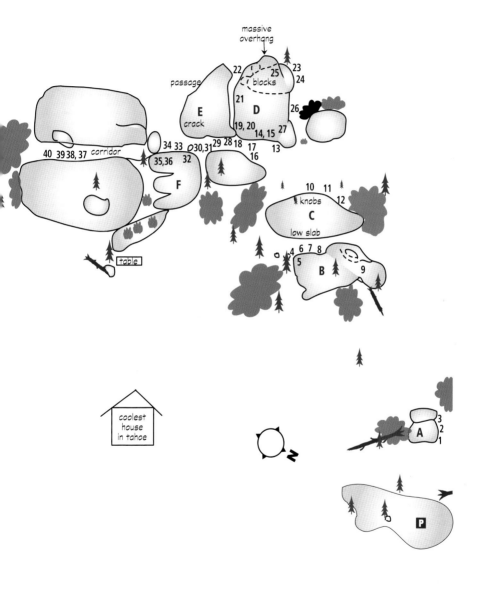

Boulder A (not shown)

❏ **1. V2** SDS to dyno at the left-hand prow.

❏ **2. V1** SDS on right-facing center crack.

❏ **3. V2** SDS at the small crack just left of where the main boulder meets the small on to its right.

Boulder B

❏ **4. V2** Jump-start off the tree root. Reachy.

❏ **5. Aggro Hippy V2** Steep prow. Start on rock below it.

❏ **6. V1** SDS at the small crack just left of the division between the main boulder and the small on to its right.

❏ **7. V4** Harder than it looks, this problem has a low start five feet right of the scoop.

❏ **8. V0** Go up the cup. Be careful on the topout; there are big jugs up there, but some of them aren't so good on top. A local guy missed the easy last move, jumped over his spotter while turning around to spot the landing, and broke his leg against the low slab behind this problem. Ouch.

❏ **9. V4** Overhung face above flat-topped boulder. Big move crux in middle.

Boulder C

❏ **10. V3** Knob mania with a stout first move dyno off two good knobs.

❏ **11. V0** Follow cool features just right of the slab.

❏ **12. VB** Good moves in the center of this slab, with a gray knob on the right side of the problem.

Boulder D

This is the goods! The biggest, proudest chunk of granite up here overhangs on three sides and all the problems are good.

13. V3 Start on a good edge down low just left of the tiny overhang. A small, square pocket marks the left side of this problem, and leads into a big move at the end.

14. V2 Sweet warmup starts at a rounded, slopey pocket below the horizontal undercling and goes to a somewhat insecure finish left of 13.

15. V2 Same start as 14, but finish between the end of 14 and the scoop, following a wide clean streak. This one's kind of squeezed in, but does feel different.

16. V2 The first move's the crux of this left-trending problem into the well-featured groove.

17. V4 A hard crimp and high step move just left of the scoop ends on a licheny slab.

18. V3 Micro-crimping just right of the corridor entrance. This thing's hard to do the same way twice—great for the Alzheimer's flash every time.

19. V3 Polish up your crack skills on this overhanging corner—it's behind you as you walk into the corridor from the front side. Good moves on good jams.

20. V5 In the corridor, traverse the small seam at eye level, being careful not to bash your head if you come off. Good moves, and it's always cool in here.

21. V7 At the end of the corridor just before the arête, there's a series of big moves on small holds guarded by a strange landing. You'll need two pads and a spotter for this one. The moves are worth it.

Boulder D (cont'd)

❑ **22. Hang Time V4**
Intimidating. Start on the
big horizontal just above the
triangle block and bucket-
haul out the big roof. Harder
if you're short. Potential for a
scary traverse left on the lip.

❑ **23. Gold's Gym V6** A classic
painful finger crack - jump
start. The sit start is really hard.

❑ **24. V9** Small edges and a
high step lead to a knob and
edge. Brutal opening move.

❑ **25. V1** Big highball. Start off
the block above 23 and 24. Traverse left as
far as you dare. The central move is hard to
reverse, so once past it you'll have to commit
to the licheny finish, adding spice to the
endeavor.

❑ **26. Project** Start on obscure holds eight
feet left of the boulder that 25 starts off,
ultimately shooting for a single gray flake
halfway up the wall, with a finish on 25.

❑ **27. The Fly V4** Another scary endeavor.
Starts by stemming between the main
boulder and a smaller one, just right of the
arête. There's a matched set of knobs in the
middle of the wall, and if you can get those
you're halfway home.

Boulder E (see map)

❑ **28. V2** Scrappy arête.

❑ **29. V0** Traverse left on crack to mantel.

Boulder F

The longest face out here, with a collection
of mediocre problems stretching from one
side to the other. The lower section drops off
a bit, making the problems longer.

❑ **30. V4** Start at a horizontal crack on the
left side of the formation below a bulge,
then fire up and left a ways to a great knob.

❑ **31. Made In the Shade V7** Horizontal
crack start, climb the
right side of the arête
on patina flake holds.
Difficult sequence getting
established above the lip.

❑ **32. V2** Start just
right of the rock in the
corridor and go up to a
big gray knob.

❑ **33. V3** Thin, slick
edges lead to a small
gray knob right of 32. It's
kinda tricky.

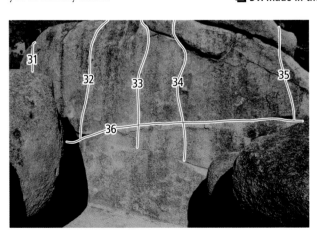

34. V2 Start left of the small boulder blocking access to the lower problems in the corridor.

35. VB Start on the small boulder and mantel up, carefully.

36. V3 Traverse the whole seam from 31 to the end of 35.

37. V3 Small edges lead up past a horizontal seam. Start on the ground uphill from the protruding rock in the corridor.

38. The Ear of Fear V3 Traverse the crack from its lowest point left into 37, then up.

39. V3 Traverse the crack until you're just downhill from the protruding rock, then head up gold edges.

40. V3 Traverse the crack all the way from the bottom to the dish downhill of 35.

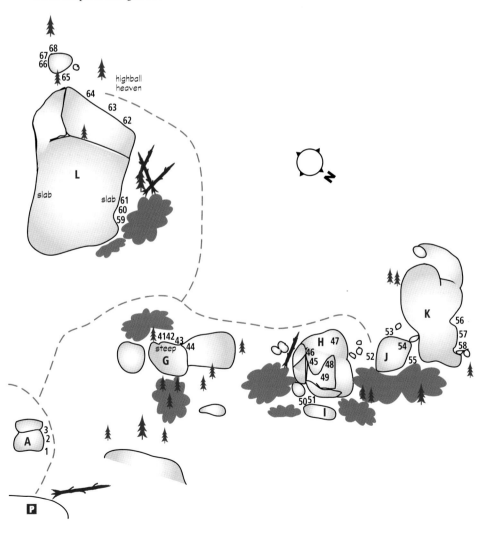

Boulder G

This is the first boulder right of A, back about 40 yards from the parking. The back side is steep and well featured, and has a tree hugging the boulder.

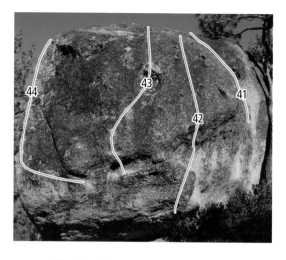

❏ **41.** V0 Jump-start if you're short, then pull into the water-carved channel

❏ **42.** V9 SDS on good edges to a powerful dyno. More hard moves to the top.

❏ **43.** V4 Grab the knobs and crank over the lip to a cool, insecure sequence involving a small knob and some cursing.

❏ **44. Project** V? Slap up the grainy arête on uncertain holds.

Boulder H

This massive, overhanging menace has nothing on the proudest side of it—not surprising given the fall, but I mean come on. Doesn't anybody have the cajones to tackle this sucker? I know I don't.

❏ **45.** V2 Serious. Slab moves six feet right of the big brown feature near the left-hand arête.

❏ **46. Project** V? Also serious. Climb the arête on the downhill side, above the terrible landing using the big feature and some stuff left of the arête.

❏ **47. Project** V? The looming, obvious highball. I don't know which is scarier: trying to flash this thing, or risking getting caught by a local while adding a toprope bolt so you don't die if you fall off. Pick your poison.

❏ **48.** V2 Unpleasant left-facing sidepull to lichen.

❏ **49.** V1 A taller start to another suspect left-facing flake.

Boulder I

This smaller block is towards the parking lot from Boulder H, and has two problems facing it.

❏ **50. V0** Cool features, cool moves.

❏ **51. V3** Nasty, frustrating little slab.

Boulder J

This low, wide boulder is the next one downhill from H, with a SDS problem facing Boulder H.

❏ **52. V2** Fun, short SDS on good knobs.

❏ **53. V3** Another short problem that's a notch harder than 52. Also good.

❏ **54. V0** Pose like a hero while following buckets along the crack.

❏ **55. V0** Balance up the bald dihedral. Hardly worth it.

Boulder K

The backside of this giant has three kinda lame problems on it. It's easier to go around to the right than the bottom.

❏ **56. VB** Follow the obvious edges on the left side of the alcove.

❏ **57. V1** Pass the creaky, crunchy overhang on either side.

❏ **58. V2** Chossy thin crack on the far left.

Boulder L

Control your mind, young Jedi - these highballs are not to be taken lightly. Start at 59 and work your way right as far as your sense of self-preservation will allow.

❏ **59. V2** Intricate, tricky slab to tall finish.

❏ **60. V1** Climb the left-facing feature.

❏ **61. V1** Head right along the handrail.

❏ **62. V4** A tough sequence at mid-height guards a seam and a spooky exit.

❏ **63. V3** This left-facing crack ends at an appalling, insecure slab sequence.

❏ **64. V2** Big holds, big moves, big air. The easiest and also the tallest of these monsters. Oh, the irony.

Boulder M

This small boulder just off the point of L has a few more problems on it.

❏ **65. V2** Slab/face climbing on small crystals facing Boulder L.

❏ **66. Project V?** RH on a flat red knob and your left on a crystal dike, then go for the top.

❏ **67. V4** Left-facing sidepulls to two white edges and a mantel.

❏ **68. V2** Grab the left-facing sidepulls, hoist your feet up and dyno for the big rail.

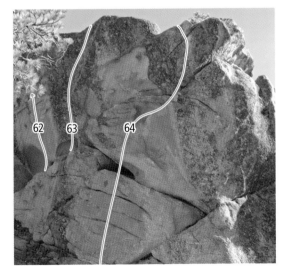

Misc. Sawmill Areas

Approach time: **1 minute**

Season: **March-December**

Number of problems: **30+**

Around Sawmill Pond and within 15 minutes of Echo View there are single boulders scattered all over, like marbles on a kitchen floor. Some have great problems on them, and all are easily accessible.

Triple Crown

Across the way from the Pie Shop area, right by the golf course and the houses, there are a few boulders. They're frustratingly blank except for a few good problems and some drilled pockets. A five-minute tour will show you everything. Don't miss the rising traverse on the far side of the largest boulder.

The Glass Boulder

This is straight across from the end of Sawmill Road where it hits Lake Tahoe Boulelvard, and there's a dirt pullout in front of it. It has six or seven problems on it, all VB-V2, but the landing's got some broken glass in it. I've seen one tribe of pad-people coming back along the trail that leads from this boulder into the archery range, and wandered out there a little, but haven't found much. Maybe there's a secret stash hiding, maybe not.

The Hemorrhoid Boulder

This boulder has nine problems from V0 to V7, and a fierce traverse that might be double digits. Park at the paved lot behind Sawmill Pond, and walk up the obvious dirt 4X4 road off the end of the parking lot. In two minutes you'll see the boulder on the right, just after the rail fence ends. It looks blocky and unassuming on the front, but the back's steep and well featured.

Along South Tahoe Boulevard back toward the Y, there's some stuff in the trees on the left (north) side of the road—the best-looking of which is .4 miles from Sawmill. This tall boulder's got eight problems on it, ranging from V1 to V6, none of them great. The line that looks best is drilled—what a waste.

Tahoe Mountain Road

Turn right onto Tahoe Mt. Road from South Lake Tahoe Boulevard and park at the first opportunity on the right by a gate. You'll see the boulders off to your left in the trees about a hundred feet away.

Show of Force

From the junction of Tahoe Mountain Road and South Tahoe Blvd, drive a quarter mile toward town on South Lake Tahoe Boulevard. and slow way down. You'll miss this thing at 40 mph, I promise. I've been here three times and keep missing it. The boulder is just off the road on the right hand side, and has a few problems on it.

Twin Peaks

This area is actually a continuation of the Pie Shop boulders, but it's far enough away to want a different description. From the junction of Sawmill Road and Highway 50, drive toward town on Highway 50. On on your left you'll see a driveway with a gate and a green transformer box below a power pole. Park here and hike straight up the hill toward a low cliff band that runs roughly parallel to 50. On the way up the hill, you'll pass two boulders on your left that have some problems, and the cliff bands themselves have a good assortment of moderate highball/toprope problems. Cross the cliff bands to your right at a break between the two, and then continue uphill and to your left until you hit three obvious, tall boulders clustered together. They've all got problems on them, some of which are fantastic.

No Name

From the Y, drive 1.2 miles and take a left onto a dirt road. A green gate and sign that reads: "Twin Peaks Area - OHV Utse" cross the road. Cross country for 100 feet until you hit a big trail. Take a left and hike west. After a couple minutes, there is a split and a

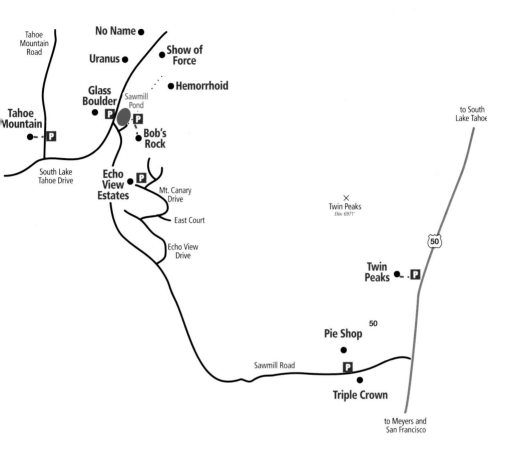

smaller trail on the right paralells the main trail. walk this small trail for a few hundred feet until it is just about to join the main trail again. hike straight up the hill for a few hundred feet and you should be able to see the boulders. There are about 30 problems.

Thunderdome

There's another objective by Echo View, with a couple short problems on it, the best of which has a shoulder-wrecking mantel for a finish. To get to this boulder, it's easiest if you park just past the junction of Echo View Drive and Canary Mtn. rather than turning onto Canary Mountain. drive. The boulder is just uphill from the road, about 40 yards in from Canary Mountain. on the right as

you drive in. Alternately, just walk down through the corridor by Boulder F at Echo View and keep trending down and right. You'll find it pretty quickly.

Bob's Rock

Approach time: **1 minute**

Season: **April-November**

Number of problems: **8**

Bob's Rock is just out of the Sawmill Pond parking lot, 30 seconds away. Park at the little dirt lot on the right just as you turn into the Sawmill Pond parking area, and your car will be pointing at the boulder. Walk up the hill trending just slightly right, and you'll be there almost immediately. Most of the problems here are tallish, so have a good spotter. The hardest line on here is a recent V9 with a wicked hard start on tiny crimps. Give it a go!

Approach

❏ **1. V1** The right hand arête as you walk up to the boulder. Good moves on good holds make this a sweet warm-up.

❏ **2. V7** This frustrating, balancy problem starts in a subtle scoop left of the arête and continues on small holds up the slab above.

❏ **3. Higher Ground V9** Start in the center of this tall face on tiny holds and tic-tac your way up more small holds. Ideal temps: 20 below. Avoid jug on Problem 2.

❏ **4. V1** The left-hand arête is pretty cool, with some technical moves down low. Be careful of the exit up high.

❏ **5. V3** Feels hard for the grade. Start about five feet left of the arête on holds that aren't as good as you'd probably like.

❏ **6. V2** Three moves will lead you onto the left side of this face to a slab finish.

❏ **7. V0** Weeble and wobble your way up the left side of this arête on good low-angle features.

❏ **8. VB** Also the downclimb big holds on a slab on the back side of the boulder by the tree.

Joe Missick on Don't get wet (underwater since 1992).
Photo by Mike Eadington

Near Kirkwood

Approach time: **1-30 minutes**

Season: **May-November**

Number of problems: **50+**

Highway 88 around
Kirkwood has a few stashes
here and there, and much
potential lurking. The
biggest collection is out near
Kirkwood Lake, scattered
down the valley from the
lake westward, and it extends
for miles: roadless, trackless
bushwhacking miles. It's
almost worth it, but not quite
– thus no development. So
if you've got an adventurous
spirit, a machete and a new
pair of Carhartts, the sky's
the limit. Otherwise, the
few things we've included
are pretty close to the road,
except for The Cube. Shrouded in myth,
legend, and misinformation, it has repelled
all who seek it.

Kevin Swift on the Birthday Boulder.

Approach

Kirkwood areas are listed in order of
appearance from Kirkwood heading north.

Birthday Boulder

First up is the Birthday Boulder, so named
because the first ascent went down on Jerry
Gillingham's birthday a few years ago. He
and Shane did most of the development out
here, so if you hit Kirkwood for a beer after
climbing. To get here, drive up 89 west to
the junction with 88 and turn right (west)
toward Kirkwood, zeroing your odometer at
the junction of Kirkwood's entrance and 88.
At .6 miles, you'll see a pullout on the right
just before a small roadcut. Park here and
walk at about 4 o'clock from your car for
five minutes along a slabby rock ridge. You'll
come to a couple of low terraces that angle
across in front of you—pick one and follow
it out left towards the skyline. You'll see the

Birthday Boulder perched on its own above
Kirkwood Lake. There are about a dozen
problems here from super easy slabs to hard
projects, and fantastic views. You can climb
here even in winter when you have to ski in.
Drive 0.1 miles farther up the road to the
turn-off for Kirkwood Lake. Take this road
down about a tenth and you'll find parking
on the left in two spots. The first one puts
you at the Gun Boulders, which sit just off
the road and trend back along the ridge
toward the Birthday Boulder. There are eight
or ten boulders lurking here, with some
absolute classics hiding out. A ten-minute
wander is guaranteed to turn up something
you'll just have to try. Go nuts because it's
all new stuff as of this writing. You can also
walk here from the Birthday Boulder and
then head back along the road. The benches
and terraces here can be a bit confusing
and cliff out and make you backtrack,
but that often just leads to more boulders
you weren't looking for. Don't come here
if you're in a hurry, the vibe here is more
casual wandering and poking around until

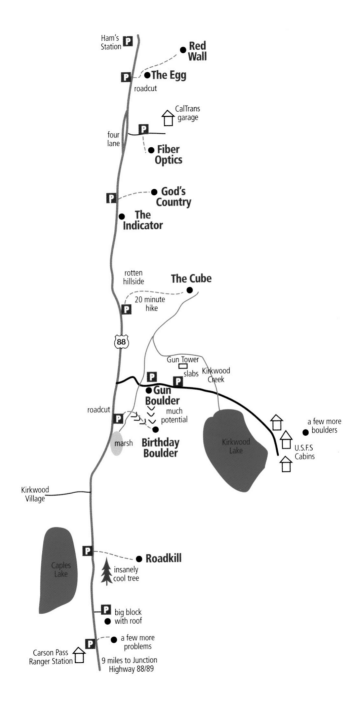

you find something great—then pour down the espresso and shoe up.

There are a couple of boulders above the cabins near the lake, but they take some finding. Take a good look out here from the Birthday Boulder first, and it will be time well spent. Be discreet when you're up here in the summer, or better yet wait until fall when conditions are perfect and the summer people are gone.

The Cube

I've only heard reports that this one exists. I've never been to it. If that doesn't have you thinking BUSHWHACK!, it should. Supposedly, this thing is pretty cool, and in a pretty cool location. It's allegedly a house-sized boulder sitting right on the edge of another cliff looking like it's ready to fall over. There are two others near it, and you can get there by parking at the second pullout on the left by the slabs (the one just after the Gun Boulders) and hiking up to the avalanche gun platform just above the slabs. From the platform you're supposed to be able to see the boulder down canyon. I wasn't able to, but that doesn't mean it's not there. Then, once you've got a sighting, you can follow the little creek that runs past the first pullout downstream to where it hits Kirkwood Creek which is the outflow from Kirkwood Lake. Follow Caples Creek downstream to where it makes a bend right, and then start trending up and left out of the creekbed on some slabs. You'll see The Cube ahead of you, along with two other boulders nearby. It sounds great, but don't say I didn't warn you... An alternate approach, shorter but more grievous, is to head up the road another mile or so and park at a big pullout on the right near a rotten, horrendous looking hillside of decomposing choss. Walk uphill a bit from the parking lot and look down the hillside to locate the boulder. There's a gully north of the parking lot that leads to a series of slabs that lead you to The Cube (again, allegedly) Should be 20 minutes: do you feel lucky, punk?

God's Country

God's Country demands some explanation. The first time Jerry and Shane came out here they saw The Indicator from the road and, bummed by the lack of features, wandered into the woods. They found three decent boulders and were chalking up when Jesus came walking by, chuffing mightily at a massive Rasta cone and throwing sticks for his two black dogs. When you get to the boulders, you'll understand how truly random such an encounter is. Naturally they said hi, and when Jesus asked what they were up to, Jerry piped up, "We're gonna climb these here rocks, man." Jesus nodded, puffed sagely again, and said, "Good for you," then walked away never to be seen again, whistling up his mutts. So it was God's Country forever after. There are a few problems here. The parking for God's Country is 8.5 miles west of Kirkwood in a pullout on the south side of the road.

The Cube

I've on
The Fiber Optics are the best boulders out here—they've got a couple of really neat problems established, and room for a few more if you pull hard. Right in the middle of the four-lane, 10.4 miles from Kirkwood, there's a turnoff for a CalTrans garage. Pull in here, park on the left, and walk back up the road the way you came, about three minutes. If you missed the boulders driving by, you won't now. There are two here, what you see is what you get, and the classic problem is the obvious one facing the road.

The phone company running fiber through here is the Volcano Telephone Company, which is funny because the day before we came out here I heard that Mount St. Helens in Washington had erupted again. I was living in Mt. Rainier the first time it blew up and have never forgotten the experience. We had to stay inside for two days to keep from breathing the ash and when we finally got to go outside it was into a world utterly devoid of color. The ground, the trees, the puddles, the grass, and houses and everything but the sky were a uniform gray, and the sky was only a little lighter shade. The only spots of color in this whole monochrome universe were people's cars, washed to keep the ash from eroding the paint. They stood out like giant jelly beans on a concrete floor. It was a very weird moment.

The Egg

Another ten miles down the road gets you to The Egg, a neat little bundle of low-ball steep problems just above the road. Getting here is a somewhat risky proposition because if you pitch off the approach you'll be lying wounded in the middle of the road. Park at the giant lot on the left looking out over the whole Mokelumne drainage, and scramble up the roadcut across the way. Just above is The Egg. The views from here are mind-blowing. On a clear day, you can literally see from Sacramento to Stockton to the East Bay and the Delta and the Coast Range and almost into Yosemite. Don't miss this, even if you never leave the ground.

From The Egg, if you walk diagonally across the hillside away from the road you'll immediately come across a few more boulders randomly scattered around, then just forest. If you take a five-minute ramble through this forest to a faint logging road and trend right, you'll come to the Red Wall, another boulder. It's got a couple decent problems on it, but more important are the truly massive pine cones you'll come across on the way. They're sugar pine cones, some a foot and a half long. They take five years of growing to drop off the tree, and will blow the mind of any city dwellers you might know. If you do take one home, pick an old one that's already done its reproductive thing. The new ones are still viable and our forests need all the help they can get.

Once you're done pulling down out here, head to Ham's Station, just two more miles along the road. Tommy runs the place and according to Shane he makes the best kamikazes within 50 miles of here, using real lime and everything. Try a Tommy Kami and see.

The Egg offers tons of features just feet from the road.

Momma Cat

Approach time: **1 minute**

Season: **yearround**

Number of problems: **11**

This boulder is named after the cat that was buried nearby. Some young person learned a hard lesson about life near here and buried their cat next to this boulder. The lesson: everybody dies eventually and what matters is what you do between now and then. So, what are you doing today? Yosemite legend TM Herbert called this "one of the best roadside boulders out there."

Getting There

This boulder is located on the north side of Highway 88 in Woodford's Canyon just west of the junction of Highway 88 and Highway 89.

Momma Cat Boulder

❏ **1. Southwest Arête** V2/V3 Start on the left side of the arête and move right.

❏ **2.** V2 Start three feet right of the arête on a big edge right of a rail/flake. Move up.

❏ **3.** V3 Start on a diagonal crack that moves right to left. Go halfway up the crack and then straight up.

❏ **4.** V2 Climb edges halfway up between diagonal crack and southeast arête.

❏ **5.** V0 Southeast arête.

❏ **6.** V0 The east side of the rock is slab with many variations.

❏ **7. Northeast Arête** V5 Awkward slaps and

Chris Ewing on Problem 8.

pulls on the right side of the arête.

❏ **8.** V4 Classic open-handed holds and edges on the middle of the northwest face.

❏ **9. Dano's Arête** V8 Climb the left side the northwest arête.

❏ **10. Tommy's Arête** V8 Climb the right side of the northwest arête on the steep gold face.

❏ **11.** V2 SDS on a left-facing sloper and crank into jugs.

Number of problems by difficulty

VB	V0	V1	V2	V3	V4	V5	V6	V7	V8	V9	V10	≥V11
0	2	0	4	1	1	1	0	0	2	0	0	0

Chris Ewing on problem 11.

Misc. Highway 88

Approach time: **1-20 minutes**

Season: **April-November**

Number of problems: **50+**

Burnside Lake

This is the place to be if you're just starting out bouldering or climbing. At the near and far-ends of the lake there is a good supply of low angle cliffs available. They are perfect for toproping, and for moderate highballs if you're solid on V0-V3 territory. The granite is all pretty good, but not as clean as some other areas that see more traffic. A little scrubbing and this will have fantastic potential.

To get here, take Highway 89 west out of Meyers and head over Luther Pass to the junction with 88. Instead of turning onto the paved roads, go straight through the intersection onto the gravel/dirt road heading roughly west. Stay on the main road until you get to Burnside Lake, which is around seven miles of washboard away. The only junction you might get fooled by is only a couple miles in at a cattle guard.

Don't take the right fork... unless you're interested in still more bouldering potential that's largely undeveloped. The boulders down the right fork are scattered all over the place and can be hard to find, but you're guaranteed to have the place to yourself. Bring your brush and check it out sometime.

Anyway, if you stay on the main road, you'll eventually drive up to the lake proper, and be presented with another choice. Just as the lake comes into view, you'll see a dirt road taking off to your right. After a couple hundred yards there's a parking spot just past a low cliff band right next to the road that might have some problems on it. If you take the curve to the right the road becomes a 4x4 road. I have no idea where it ultimately goes.

Park at the pullout and walk past the dead end that's straight ahead, then start angling up and right as the terrain allows, roughly following the back side of a low ridge. After five minutes you'll see a cliff band above you to the right, with a couple of boulders on the left side of it. That's one area of interest.

The other has an easier approach with great problems, but it's closer to the lake and solitude isn't assured. Whatever, it's still good stuff up here. Park at the lake, and at the far end of the parking lot there is a boulder with a few things on it. From this boulder, head left up the hill towards the obvious, clearly visible cliffbands. Pick a line, any line—you can't go wrong. A half rope and a half rack with get you all the topropes you can stand, and a good pad and spot will turn this place into highball heaven. Perfect for a day of relaxed mileage.

Misc. Woodford's

Tired of granite? Can't stand the thought of another perfect sloper, edge or knob? Come down here and get some sandstone, or crank big moves on ridiculously steep, creaky, volcanic choss. There isn't a huge concentration of problems here, but you can pull granite, sandstone, and basalt just a few minutes apart and get a break from the steady diet of granite in the basin.

There's another river to play in, Grover Hot Springs for a soak, and Sorensen's for tasty (pricey) food. Don't forget the always enticing thought of spying an inspiring line from the boulders, then staggering miles up one of the godforsaken hillsides toting your whole rack, only to find out the only good line up there's already been done. In the seventies. With EBs and hexes. My favorite.

Everything in Woodford's has the potential to be perfect in all sorts of conditions. Almost anything short of a winter storm can be weathered and bouldered in down here in the rain shadow. Bring a tarp and some extra clothes, a thermos of espresso, and some bakery items – enough sugar and you're golden.

The approach is trivial (unless the road's closed for a blizzard, when you'll be snowboarding anyway). Take 89 west out of Meyers, turn left at the junction with 88 and head down the hill. You'll pass Sorensens, and then the boulders will start to appear.

The first is a massive chunk of stone just off the road on your left side as you're headed downhill. It's got a tree growing in front of it and it's split all the way through by a wide crack. It's also too tall for anything but terrifying problems, except for the inside of the boulder.

It's split in an L-shape, which you can enter on the right side, and in the crook of the L there are a couple cool cracks that you can boulder up inside a giant chimney feature. Also, some stuff has been bolted, so if you're into topropes you can find them too.

Then you'll come to The Grotto, or rather, the parking lot for it. Once you pass the bunker boulder, you'll head downhill to a bridge. Cross the bridge, turn around, and park on the right side a little short of the bridge in a smallish pullout. From here, The Grotto is at 2 o'clock to the front of your car, about a 15 minute walk up the hill. Cross the small ravine to your right, bushwhack a short way up the hill and you'll hit a faint trail cutting across the hillside. Take this trail up and left, and the first obvious objective you'll come to is the White Wave, a great V3 that traverses from the lower right to upper left of a boulder shaped like a breaking wave.

Next up is Bertha's Boulder—another huge block, this one with a weird survivalist-type bunker built underneath it. There isn't too much here. There are a couple problems, a wide crack, and an aid line that supposedly goes free around 5.12 something.

There are other scattered problems in the small collection of rocks near The Wave, and more up the hill behind it in a band that might go all the way to the crest of the hill. The rock's pretty good, and there might be more potential up there.

Hangman's Cave

Take 88 past Markleville and about five minutes out of town you'll start to see some rock formations near the road. Slow way down and start looking right. About 50 feet above the road, just before Hangman's Bridge, you'll see a low cave partially hidden

by trees with a dirt road leading t[o] there are a zillion holds, almost as m[a] bolts, and plenty of potential for bould[e] Bring extra pads 'cause everything's tall, a[n] maybe lead stuff first if it's near your limit.

Rumors abound of more problems out here, and I'm sure they're all true. A quick hike off the road almost anywhere between the beginning of the canyon and the intersection at Woodford's will probably yield a boulder or two, not to mention the ridiculous profusion scattered along the hills to either side of 89 below the cliffbands. You'd get some big legs bagging all these, and big lungs, too.

HIGHWAY 88

it. Inside
ny.
ring.
d.

into problems
that give good value and take a while
to crack. Think pain. Think frustration,
shredded tips, convoluted sequences, and
abraded palms. This place rules the Tahoe
scene. It has better problems than almost
anywhere else, a minimal approach, and
great stone. Problems here range from VB
to V9 with some potential remaining for
really hard-core boulderers. The climbing
here tends to be fingery, with great landings
on compacted sand. There are four areas
here: North, Middle, South and the Ladder
Boulder area.

North is the area closest to Tahoe City,
South closest to Emerald Bay. Middle is
between them, and the Ladder area includes
a boulder at the entrance to D. Bliss State
Park proper, the Ladder Boulder itself, and
a couple of smaller rocks below the Ladder.
Come out when it's cold if you've got a
project here and everything will feel a grade
easier. If it's hot out, you're suffering. Better
to join your dog at the creek crossing on the
way to Middle Bliss.

Ludde Hagberg on a V2 arête.

Driving Directions

To get here from South Lake, take 89 west
towards Tahoe City. At the Eagle Falls
trailhead (on the south side of the road)
zero your odometer. In 1.8 miles you will
come to the parking for South Bliss at the
first sandy roadcut you come to.

From North Tahoe, take 89 East towards

Tahoe and zero your odometer at the Meek's
Bay Fire Station. At 4.6 miles, you'll see the
North Bliss parking area with an electrical
junction box at the north end of it.

Once you're at either end of the
bouldering areas, the inset map will guide
you.

Parking isn't a problem here. You can
always find a pullout within walking
distance.

Approach

Each area has an individual approach
explanation before the problem descriptions.
They're all minimal and painless.

Number of problems by difficulty

VB	V0	V1	V2	V3	V4	V5	V6	V7	V8	V9	V10	≥V11
7	25	20	19	19	8	8	6	2	0	1	0	0

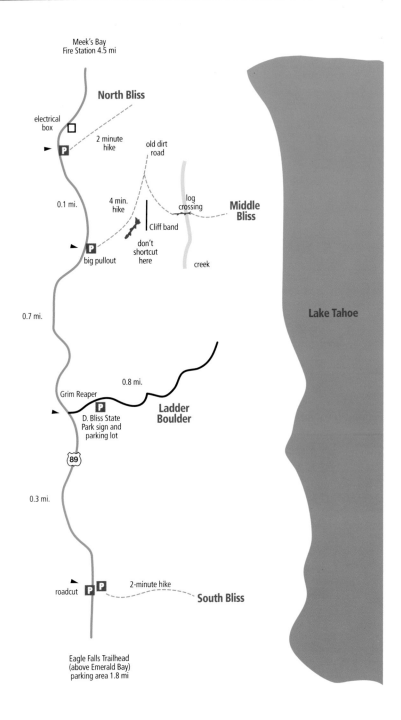

Meek's Bay
Fire Station 4.5 mi

North Bliss

electrical
box

2 minute
hike

old dirt
road

4 min.
hike

0.1 mi.

log
crossing

**Middle
Bliss**

Cliff band

don't
shortcut
here

big pullout

creek

Lake Tahoe

0.7 mi.

0.8 mi.

Grim Reaper

**Ladder
Boulder**

D. Bliss State
Park sign and
parking lot

89

0.3 mi.

2-minute hike

roadcut

South Bliss

Eagle Falls Trailhead
(above Emerald Bay)
parking area 1.8 mi

Ladder Boulder

Fantastic jug-hauling galore. Drive in the entrance of D.L. Bliss State Park and follow the road down 0.8 miles. At the last turn before the pay station, you'll see the backside of the Ladder Boulder on the right. It won't look like anything worth checking out, but you're looking at the wrong side. Walk around the corner and it all makes sense.

It is illegal to park next to the boulder. Please pay the $3 day use fee to keep good climber/ranger relations.

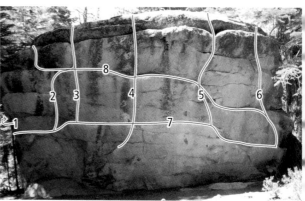

❏ **1. V1** Grab jugs and haul yourself up just around the left corner.

❏ **2. Ladder Left V3** Start in the alcove and pass a small dyno on big holds, then exit to the right.

❏ **3. V2** Grab the obvious edge at face-height and go for two more edges that are bigger and better than they look, finish on 2.

❏ **4. Left Side Dyno V4** SDS at a great sidepull, establish on any of the edges, and throw a long way to the hugest bucket you'll ever miss. Good fun.

❏ **5. Regular Route V2** More bomber holds lead straight up through a V-shaped notch.

❏ **6. V3** Climb the far right side of the overhang on good holds to a less than secure mantel.

❏ **7. Low Traverse V4** Traverse the entire boulder from a SDS at the far right side into Problem 1 and finish up 1. The lower of the two traverses.

❏ **8. V3** Traverse from the middle of 6 into the short crack system left of the end of 2. High traverse.

Grim Reaper

Just below and 50 feet north of the main entrance parking area (just off 89) is a classic, square-cut dihedral with a thin crack capped by a roof. Clean and classic V3.

Stepping Stones

From the Ladder Boulder, walk northeast on the hiking trail (sorta toward Lake Tahoe). After a few hundred feet, there is a boulder on your left and then one on your right. Both are a little dirty but have some good VB-V3 problems. From here, leave the trail and walk east (toward Lake Tahoe). After 100 feet, you come to the Stepping Stones: a collection of about 15 quality problems ranging from VB to V-really-hard-project. There is a great handrail traverse, some cool highballs, a nice crack, and a number of projects.

Mark's Roof

From the Ladder Boulder, walk southwest on the hiking trail for a few hundred feet. You will see a rad roof boulder up on the hill on your left. This has a great V7.

South Bliss

This is the trailer park cousin of the other Bliss areas, with fewer problems that generally aren't as good. Much of the rock here is grainy and decomposing, but the problems included below are pretty good. You can find more here if you're willing to bushwhack or settle for poorer rock.

The Hueco Boulder

This is the first boulder you come to, with large huecos facing the trail. The left-hand problem tends to spit everybody off in the same place. Do some lat pulldowns at the gym before you get on it. Around the corner to the left from problem 1 is a V4 pad stack, grainy face. Also problems 1 and 2 can be reduced to an enjoyable V0 warm up with a pad stack.

❏ **1. V3, V7** Either take a very high start up and left from the center hueco for the easy problem, or start low in the hole for a much harder one on worse holds.

❏ **2. V3** Same starting hueco, but go up and right on interesting edges and slopes. Height dependent also.

❏ **3. V0** Pull onto the dished slab on the right side of the face and it's almost over.

❏ **4. VB** The slab right of the last huecos.

Boulder B

The smooth overhanging face right of A has some fragile, crunchy flakes on the front of it that might yield a problem—at least until everything broke.

Battle Cry Boulder

This boulder has got a tree hugging the left side of it, and some cool problems waiting to go up.

❏ **5. Project V?** With some srubbing, this bald slab left of the tree might go on imaginary holds.

❏ **6. Project V?** There's some possible micro-edging just right of the tree.

❏ **7. Battle Cry V6** On the slab side of the arête, pad stack to gain the arête with your left hand and a micro razor with your right. Then balance your way up this classic arête.

❏ **8. Project V?** Delicate, desperate face just right of the arête.

❏ **9. V5** Hard moves up a slopey, right-facing sidepull with bad feet.

❏ **10. V2** Right-facing edges to a bulge. Watch the landing on this one because the sloping boulder is classic ankle-breaker material.

Thiry yards northwest of Boulder C is a boulder with a fallen dead tree next to it. Straight up the middle/right is "Olde English" V5. The problem to the left is undone.

Boulder D

❏ **11. Rusty Nail** V2 Great edging up the patina flakes.

❏ **12. Solar Eclipse** V4 Start low on the edge and work your way out the bulge to a spicy topout. Fantastic quality, heart-fluttering finish, great view, what's not to like?

❏ **13.** V4 Same start, but escape left onto 11 at the bulge instead of finishing straight up. Still good, but less manly.

Boulder E

There's not as much as you'd think in this big cluster of boulders, but there is one massively proud highball waiting to go down. It will need some brushing, and many pads, Looks stout.

❏ **13.** V? This will be hard and scary.

❏ **14.** V3 SDS. Small, crumbly, crummy.

Boulder F

Directly behind you when you're facing Boulder D is a cool boulder. the boulders are 15 feet apart and the problems face south. The "Griffolator" is the right problem, V4, It starts in huecos and moves left to a shallow corner with flakes. The "Thugolator" is the left problem and it's a direct start to Griffolator and its V6.

Boulder G

This huge boulder sits in the middle of the ravine, below the level of E. On the right side of the pretty, streaked face there's a stepped slab with some features on it.

❏ **15. Project**

Boulder H

Across the ravine there are some crack problems, two of which are really good. Just look for the obvious clean crack that faces your side of the ravine.

❏ **16.** V2 Ring-locks to rattly hands on a steep, straight in crack. Too bad it's so short.

❏ **17.** V? Project. Face climb the seam and edges just left of the OW.

❏ **18.** V2 Scabby, nasty off-width splitting the rock. Maybe with some brush work this will be a new classic...or not.

❏ **19.** V3 Another classic crack problem. Tight hands to fists over a bulge. Good quality, rough landing.

After crossing the ravine, walk 75 yards south to a proud boulder pearched on a sandy ledge. The arête with the dike halfway up is "Quiver me timbers" V4 and the overhanging face to the right is "Ho-Ho Man" V7. These problems are good, probably the best after you cross the ravine.

Middle Bliss

This is the best that Bliss has to offer. If you boulder V6 or less, you'll be well served here, and probably go home with your tips looking medium-rare. You can construct a fantastic circuit of moderates here, and all the landings are great.

Boulder A

The first boulder you come to walking up the approach trail has a bunch of good moderates on it. The V2 on the back side left of the tree is the best of them.

❏ **1. V2** Start on the rightfacing sidepull and dyno for the giant bucket. About the third time you miss, your tips will be shredded. Ahhh, Bliss.

❏ **2. V2** Start on a right-facing sidepull and haul yourself up to the jugs.

❏ **3. V3** Start on a hueco and go for the slopers and then the buckets. You gotta want it.

❏ **4. V2+** If you start low, V5 if you sit down. The SDS is aggravating and adds little value.

❏ **5. V2** Start left of 4, using the edge of the prow, then slap your way up and right.

❏ **6. Celebrity Victim V6** SDS on the low arête. Hard slopers, with much trickery needed.

❏ **7. V0** Right side of face, starting at an oddly shaped pocket.

❏ **8. V0** Left side of face, same start,

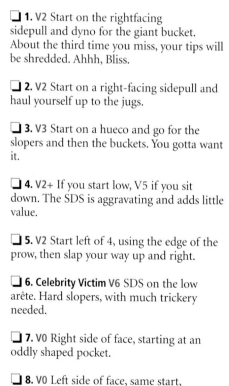

balancey.

Boulder B

Small boulder left of the Brain.

❏ **9. V0** Uninspiring, licheny slab on the left.

❏ **10. V0** More of the same, in the middle.

❏ **11. V0** A little better, on the right side.

❏ **12. V3** SDS cool traverse from right to left with a big move in the middle.

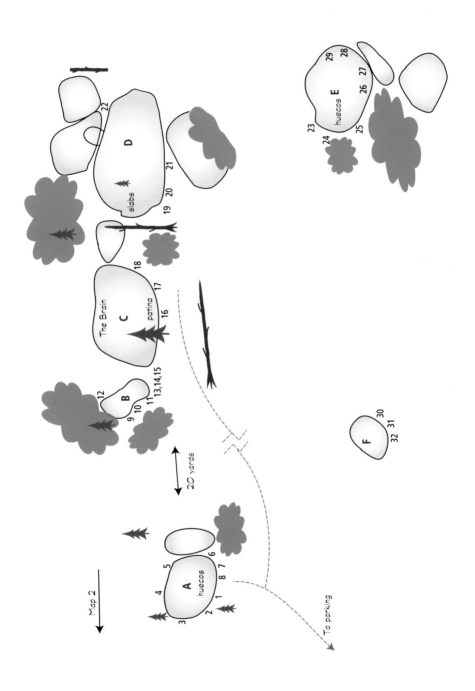

The Brain (Boulder C)

This is the warm-up boulder (if you don't mind high problems), with many moderate problems on great tortoiseshell patina. It's got the huge tree right in front, with a log for easy spectator seating.

❏ **13.** V0 Up the arête and around the corner – follow the magic huecos.

❏ **14.** V1 Start at 14, then follow a rising traverse above the seam. No chimneying behind the tree, either.

❏ **15.** V2 Same start, but traverse low on the seam and finish on 16.

❏ **16.** V0 Grab the obvious edges just right of the tree and head up.

❏ **17.** V1 The nubbly, polished face right of 16 has an insecure, slabby problem that requires more precision than you'd expect.

❏ **18.** VB this slab is also the down route, with many possible variations.

The aspect of the Brain opposite these problems has many slab variations on it.

Boulder D

The large boulder uphill and to the Brain's right, with two little trees growing on top of it.

❏ **19.** V2 Face just right of the arête. Athletic start, good holds higher up.

❏ **20.** V5 This one will test your crimp strength and high-stepping ability. It's just right of 19, and has a difficult start.

❏ **21.** V2 Good problem, but the landing gets worse as you climb higher. Follow the edges and knobs starting where the two boulders start to converge.

❏ **22.** V5 SDS. This short problem is on the small block just behind C, facing towards it. Have a spotter for your head.

Boulder E

Another tall boulder, but this one has no trees on top. It's about 100 feet up and right from D. Good problems, some are kinda heady near the end.

☐ **23. V0** Tall, well-featured rounded prow.

☐ **24. V3** Height dependent – fold and staple yourself into the scoop, then stretch out again on the slabby upper section. Or the other way around if you're short.

☐ **25. V3** Start in the huecos just right of the prow on the front of the boulder, then step around to the front at mid-height, or go straight up right for a burly finish.

☐ **26. V2** Face just left of the right-hand prow. This is a classic that's easier up high, but no give-away. If you start off the block it's around V1.

☐ **27. V0** Arête, good moves, bad landing.

☐ **28. V3** Difficult sidepulling gets you a licheny topout.

☐ **29. V3** Left leaning arête, strange, slopey hands but good feet. Needs cleaning.

Boulder F

This small boulder is on the right as you approach and has three okay problems on it.

☐ **30. V0**

☐ **31. V0**

☐ **32. V0**

Big Face

Some of you have seen pictures on the internet, others have scammed beta out of V-Boulder magazine (R.I.P.). No flash for you! Anyway, it's pretty cool, and pretty tall.

☐ **33. VB** Buckets right of the rounded arête. The down route if you're running laps.

☐ **34. V0** SDS to jugs straight up the arête.

☐ **35. Big Face V1** Regular start is V1. Direct is V4 on sharpish edges. Either way, it's a great problem on bomber holds.

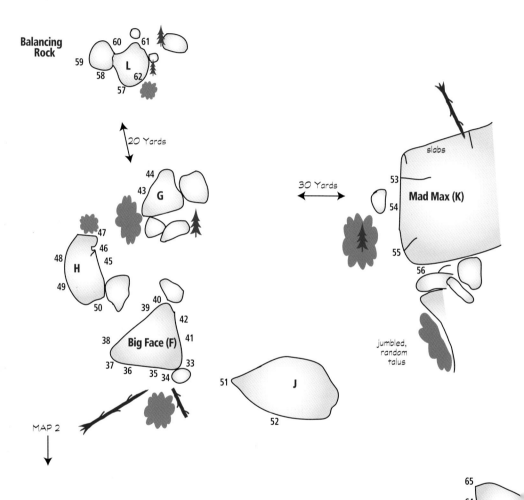

Balancing Rock

60 61

59

L

58 62

57

20 Yards

44
43 G

47
46
48 45
H
49
50

40
39
42
Big Face (F) 41
38
37 36 35 34 33

51
J
52

MAP 2

slabs

30 Yards

53
Mad Max (K)
54

55

56

jumbled, random talus

65
64
63
The Pyrami

36. V9 Hard pulling on tiny edges right of arête.

37. V4 The stellar, obvious arête. Tallish.

38. V1 Start as if trying the arête, then escape left up the face. Still strange, but way easier.

39. V1 Lieback the outside of the dihedral to a slab finish.

40. V1 This spooky dihedral's not to be taken lightly. While not difficult, it does demand some mind control.

41. VB Follow the seam.

42. VB Clamber up the outside corner right of the buckets. Short.

Boulder H

This boulder only has one problem on it right now, and it's a Tahoe Basin must-do.

43. V5 A strong, totally independent line with no variations or sit-downs or traverses included. I love it. Plus, the top's high and insecure—even better.

44. Project V? There's a hard problem lurking here on tiny holds, just waiting for some steel-tendoned warrior to crush it.

Boulder I

This small block has a few strange problems on it. None of them are great, but they'll sucker you in, promising a quick few moves. Don't be fooled, they're all kinda weird. Not hard, just weird.

45. V0 Climb face left of crack.

46. V0 Work the seam, baby, work it.

47. V2 SDS on arête.

48. V0 Thin edges up a short face.

49. V1 Bald slab. Try this one with no hands, and do your best impression of Shaolin-style Drunken Boxing.

50. V0 Another bald slab, easier than 46, but will still require much body English to send with no hands. This is the downclimb.

Boulder J

This immense block only has two problems on it, one of which is an area test-piece in every sense of the word. The ship's prow feature is proud, but really dangerous. There's a back-breaker in the landing zone that no amount of padding can eliminate. Proceed with caution.

❏ **51. V?** I've heard everything from V5 to V8 for this problem. It's an incredibly aesthetic line, but you've gotta be willing to suffer for what you love if you want this one. It looks plenty hard, and I'll be damned if I'm going to get on it without a rope. Find out for yourself.

❏ **52. V2** Slab moves right of the arête. While nowhere near as classic, you'll live if you pitch off this one.

Mad Max (Boulder K)

I loved the movie the first time I saw it, and the same's true of this big mutha's namesake problem. It's too bad this gets done so little, as the holds might be dusty when you get on it. Don't worry, with a little cleaning it's wicked cool.

❏ **53. V4** Take the right leaning crack as high as you dare, then bawl for a toprope, quick.

❏ **54. Mad Max V6** A classic. Grab the opposing sidepulls, huck for the seam, then traverse right to the crack. Remember to slide your crashpad right as the slug-fest continues to a J-Tree-type exit.

❏ **55. V2** Flaring crack, a little grainy and insecure at the finish.

❏ **56. Project V?** Around the corner from 50 there's a lieback flake that just might gain some holds farther right. The key word is might.

Boulder L

This balancing rock assemblage seems to have been neglected. Most of what's here is waiting for somebody to scrub it so we can all get after it.

❏ **57. V5** Palm your way up this strange, gritty bulge and beach yourself on the mantel above it.

❏ **58. Project V?** Pull over the lip on bad holds just left of the crack.

❏ **59. Project V?** This will be an impressive send. Follow the dike up and right with terrible feet.

❏ **60. Project V?** Crank up an improbable series of tiny holds, trying not to fall back against the rock behind you.

❏ **61. V?** Okay edges lead up and left past the overhang. It's kind of a hassle with the smaller boulder in the way.

❏ **62. VB** Slab moves just left of the small tree will get you in brushing position for the other problems.

The Pyramid (M)

This balancing rock assemblage seems to have

❏ **63. V?** Right variation to 64. Looks wicked.

❏ **64. Head Bangers Fall V6** Start on the jug in a scoop, get standing on jug and traverse left to the arête on friction moves. Then climb the scary but easy blank slab up and right or escape left.

❏ **65. Knob Roulette V1** Mantel the big knob, then climb the slab or escape left.

❏ **66. V?** Overhanging face with a few holds. Might go.

North Bliss

North Bliss is great: the approach is minimal and the location is cool, the landings are flat, and all the problems are clustered really close together. Don't miss the Asteroid Boulder. If you dare, there's a creaky, crunchy highball of doom waiting to go up on one side of the balancing rock. Now, THAT would be proud! If it falls over and squashes you like Indiana Jones, don't blame me. Once you're done pulling down, roam around the campground at night making bear sounds and then plunder all the abandoned picnic coolers.

Boulder A

Slabby boulder with a tree on the right side.

❏ **1. V0** Start behind the tree, being careful not to break any of the branches. Follow the seam up and left.

❏ **2. V2** Head up the dihedral left of the tree.

❏ **3. V4** This slabby start is harder than it looks. Prepare for frustration.

❏ **4. V1** Go straight up the prow on tiny

holds.

❏ **5. V1** Follow the sloping holds on the slab, and keep your feet weighted.

❏ **6. V1** There's another slab left of 5 – also low-angle and worth doing.

❏ **7. V1** Yet another slab, where the boulder behind this one starts to form a corridor.

The Meteorite Boulder

This thing's so cool. There are a bunch of good problems here, and if you're strong you can tick them all one after another for a brutal, forearm torching workout.

❏ **8. V1** This is a comical two-move problem. Start on the knob and crank onto the slab, grinding your knees to hamburger if you botch the move.

❏ **9. Spiderman V7** Classic. If you've got the guns, you simply have to do this route. Many holds converge at a razor crimp guarded by a confusing sequence below.

❏ **10. V5** Edges to a difficult slab/smear sequence. Seldom done due to a spooky, insecure top-out.

❏ **11. V4** Start just right of 10, going up and right past two small knobs to another insecure slab finish.

❏ **12. V6** Same start as 10, but traverse left at mid-height and finish on The Asteroid. This one doesn't feel much easier than The Asteroid.

❏ **13. V2** Pad stack start to knobs on the slab at the far right side of the Asteroid wall.

❏ **14. V3** Right facing sidepull on the prow.

❏ **15. V1** Tricky slab.

❏ **16. V1**

18,19,20

17   21

Boulder C

Big boulder with a small tree growing out of a crack on the right side.

❏ **17. V7** off the ground, V3 jumpstart on the arête, then follow the seam. Good problem.

❏ **18. V3** Mantel the loose flake, and try not to rip it off in the process.

❏ **19. V2** Start low on the hollow, creaky rail and go up and left to the edges. Pull down, not out.

❏ **20. V3** Traverse sloping arête/edge to the right.

❏ **21. Project V?** There's something here that almost went this year, on small strange holds that lead to a mantel, just left of where the boulder curves toward 20.

Boulder D

Here are some OK warm-ups, which feel harder than they probably are. It helps to know the sequences (surprise.) The arête near the tree is the best of them.

❏ **22. V3** SDS on flake to slopey buckets.

❏ **23. V0** The huecos.

❏ **24. V2** SDS, V0 stand start.

❏ **25. V0** Great overhanging arête, finish up and left for full value, or escape right.

❏ **26. V7** Fiendish small crimps and bad feet on the left-hand arête.

❏ **27. V0** Pad stack or V4 low start on insecure holds.

❏ **28. V5** Sidepulls and slopers up into the lichen. Low percentage, low value.

❏ **29. V4** Obvious edges to insecure, slopey finish. Also low percentage, but more satisfying. Reach higher than you think you'll have to, and it will be easier.

Boulder E

Grainy split boulder, left of C as you walk in.

❏ **30. V3** Patina start to sloping edges.

❏ **31. V0** SDS on the central crack.

❏ **32. V0** Just right of the crack.

Boulder F

This boulder's cracked all the way through.

❏ **33. V2** SDS to a crack.

❏ **34. VB** Slab.

❏ **35. V0** Good steep handcrack

These next boulders don't have photos or topos, and aren't as good.

Boulder G

The first boulder on the left as you hike in.

❏ **36. V2** Strange mantel on the bulge - don't scrape your nipples off if you fall.

❏ **37. V0** Slab.

Boulder H

First boulder on the right as you hike in, looking down into the ravine

❏ **38. V3** Left-trending slopes above a slab lead to extremely fragile flakes.

❏ **39. Project V?** Delicate slab moves on tiny, breakable holds just right of the arête.

Boulder I

Across the ravine from the parking lot is an obvious tall, tapering boulder.

❏ **40. V2** Arête - hard start and tall finish.

❏ **41. Project V?** Hyper-delicate cranking on tiny edges – send this, get sponsored.

❏ **42. Project V?** Hard sidepulls on a flake to a desperate topout.

North Bliss

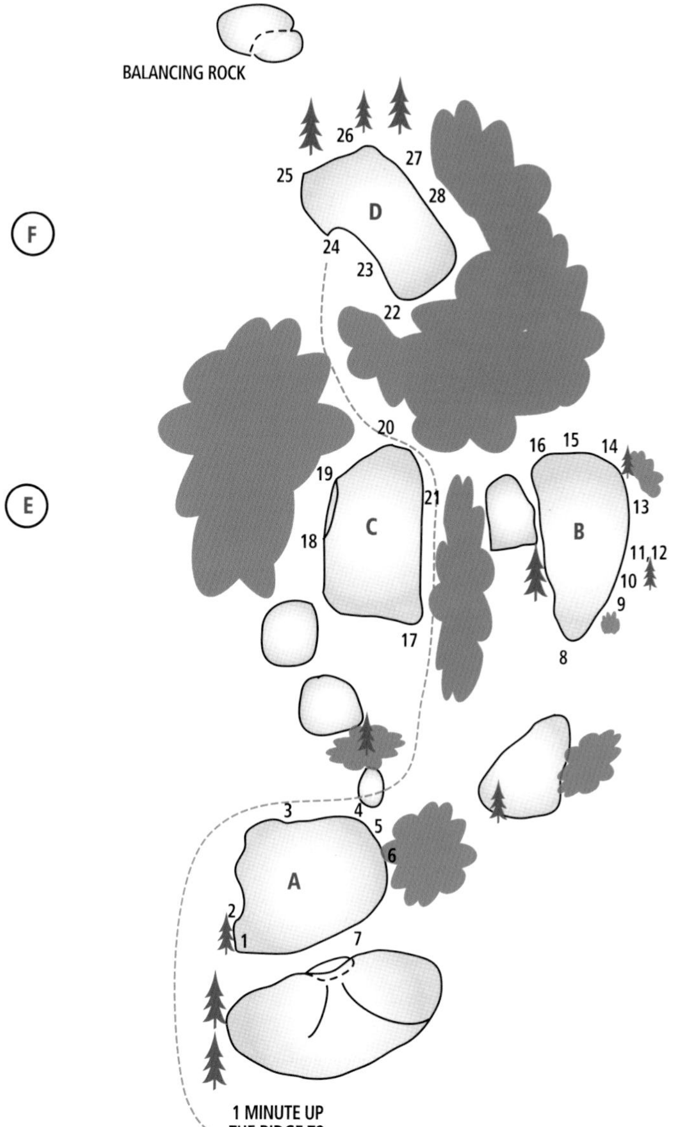

BALANCING ROCK

D

25
26
27
28
24
23
22

20
19
21
C
18
17

16 15 14
13
B
11 12
10
9
8

3
4
5
6
A
2
1
7

1 MINUTE UP
THE RIDGE TO

P

F

E

G

H

Old County

Approach time: **5 minutes**

Season: **April-November**

Number of problems: **104**

This is a nice change of pace: volcanic rock. The Old County boulders are the same welded tuff as the Big Chief climbing area, and make for a totally different style of climbing than the familiar granite found elsewhere. This stuff is one giant hold, every inch of which is probably climbable at one grade or another. It's also wicked sharp. If you can stand the loss of friction and sensitivity, it's worth taping all your tips before starting your session if you have any interest in climbing tomorrow. The pointy, discontinuous nature of the features makes for interesting beta. There are Spock holds, rotary phone dials, Boy Scout salutes, and some that feel like grabbing the lower canines of a howler monkey – how you place your fingers is as important as where.

Driving Directions

From Tahoe City, drive east on Highway 28 toward King's Beach. After a mile and a half, you'll pass a 7-Eeven on the right, and in another .6 miles you will encounter the turnoff for Old County Road. Follow Old County uphill until it dead-ends at the T intersection with Beverly Road, which goes uphill to the left. Park at this deadend, by a pre-school that looks like somebody's house. NOTE: it is VERY important to be sensitive to the neighbors when parking. Be as low key as possible. If you see a lot of other cars parked, then drive back down the street and look for parking that will be the least noticed by the neighbors. Access to this area depends on climbers keeping a low profile.

Approach

Walk past the back yard/playground. It has a bunch of cut-off log rounds standing on end marking the edge of the yard. Just past the house, there will be a single-track leading up and left. Take this and at the first major trail junction (actually an old road), turn left. You should be seeing the boulders now, and going left will get you the main trail into the area, which is on the right after about 40 yards. This path will take you right to the lower boulders. There are more higher up the hillside, and even a cliff band if you are willing to bushwhack far enough.

Number of problems by difficulty (including Upper Old County and Binder)

VB	V0	V1	V2	V3	V4	V5	V6	V7	V8	V9	V10	≥V11
13	23	24	16	14	9	10	7	3	0	0	0	0

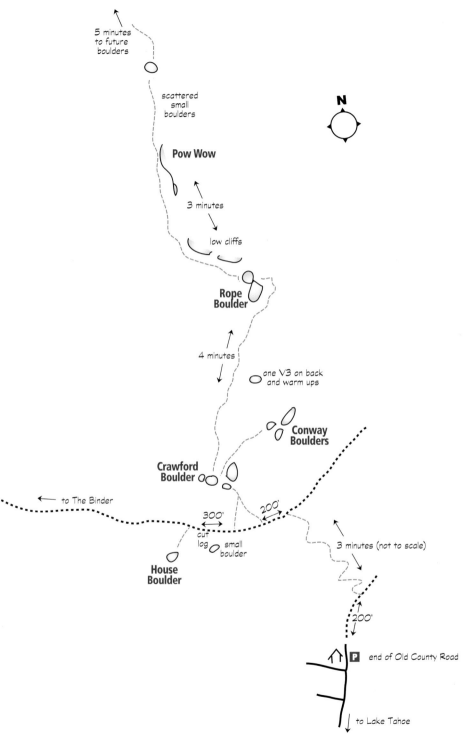

5 minutes
to future
boulders

scattered
small
boulders

Pow Wow

3 minutes

low cliffs

**Rope
Boulder**

4 minutes

one V3 on back
and warm ups

**Conway
Boulders**

**Crawford
Boulder**

← to The Binder

300'

200'

cut
log   small
boulder

3 minutes (not to scale)

**House
Boulder**

200'

end of Old County Road

to Lake Tahoe

N

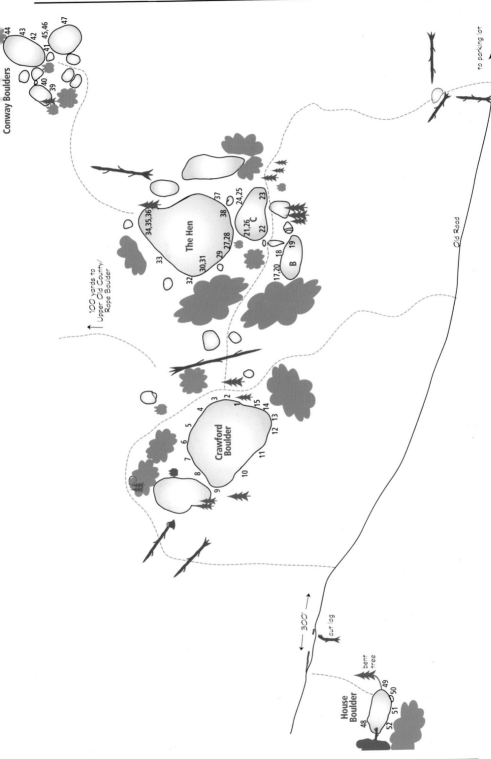

The Crawford Boulder

The Crawford Boulder is the first one you come to on the main trail. It's got a bunch of good moderates on it, and an easy walk down the back side.

❏ **1.** V3 Stylish moves from a right-facing crimp up through a yellow lichen streak, this is the first obvious problem right of the tree as you're facing the boulder.

❏ **2.** V5 Tiny holds lead up and left into 1, starting five feet left of the crack.

❏ **3.** V2 SDS Start at the right-facing crack just left of the blunt arête and finish on the slab.

❏ **4.** V1 Slab problem on rounded arête.

❏ **5.** V1 Crimp and high-step past small, fiddly holds up the slab.

❏ **6.** V3 Small nubbins on a bulge lead to still more slabbiness.

❏ **7.** V5 SDS. Grab the right-facing edges and toss for the sloping end of a crack. Sweet.

❏ **8.** V6 SDS at a small seam and go for a good edge out left.

❏ **9.** V6 SDS at a right-facing triangular edge and claw over the bulge on broken holds.

❏ **10.** V1 Mossy mantel.

❏ **11.** V1 Another mossy problem on edges and pockets.

❏ **12.** VB Follow a crack to slab moves.

❏ **13.** V1 Sweet moves over a bulge on pockets, edges and knobs.

❏ **14.** V2 One move off a deep pocket, then mantel.

❏ **15.** V7 SDS. Hard moves on small holds through a bulge eight feet left of the tree.

❏ **16.** V2 Good edges and slopes to crack, starting just left of the tree.

Boulder B

This small boulder on the south side of the trail has three short problems and a traverse.

❏ **17. VB** Far right side by the bushes.

❏ **18. V2** SDS on undercling flake.

❏ **19. V0** Mantel on the left side.

❏ **20. V2** Low traverse from 17 to 19.

Boulder C

This boulder holds a great traverse that goes almost all the way around it. It's not tall enough for much else, though.

❏ **21. VB** Knobs just right of the notch between boulders.

❏ **22. VB** Mantel.

❏ **23. V0** Mantel the arête by the small tree.

❏ **24. V0** Pull up into the groove.

❏ **25. V5** Start on a bad right-facing sloper, and go to small edges and pockets.

❏ **26. V6** Traverse the entire boulder from 21 to the end of 25.

The Hen

Another massive chunk of volcanic fun, directly across from A.

❏ **27. V5-V7** Height dependent traverse right, from a small edge at waist height to a tiny edge/pocket sequence.

❏ **28. V5** Start on the same hold as 27, go up to small pockets.

❏ **29. V4** SDS on undercling to an obvious round pocket.

❏ **30. V4** Tiny holds lead right above 29.

❏ **31. V1** Up the crack.

❏ **32. V2** Small edges up to right end of tiny roof.

❏ **33. V1** Pull straight up over the center of the tiny roof.

❏ **34. V0** Crack to slab.

❏ **35. V4** Low traverse from 34, finish on 31.

❏ **36. V1** High traverse from 34 to far right side of the tiny roof and up.

❏ **37. V7** Sick sloper and razor crimp on prow to mossy topout.

❏ **38. V5** SDS is a height dependent project. Start on slopey, right-facing sidepull and go up to smallish holds.

Conway Boulders

The Conway Boulders have a few good problems and one project. You can see them from on top of the Crawford Boulder. Head right from The Hen Boulder about 100 feet on a small trail and you'll be there.

Boulder A

This boulder is on the left as you walk in.

❏ **39.** VB Slab with good edges 10 feet right of the tree.

❏ **40.** V2 A good SDS on a right-facing undercling face has fun moves.

Boulder B

This is the best boulder in this section. The traverse hasn't gone yet. Mike Eadington nearly ticked it a few years ago, but broke off a crucial foothold after falling on the last move the try before. Brutal.

❏ **41.** V? Project. The Tape Traverse starts on the far left side of this boulder and heads right across the entire face before topping out on Problem 4. Sharp and worthy.

❏ **42.** V2 Start in the obvious round hueco and head straight up on good holds.

❏ **43.** V3 Pockets and sidepulls just right of a half-buried flake at ground level. Go up and slightly right.

❏ **44.** V2/3 On the right side of the boulder, start on a big right-facing flake and pull over the top in a few moves.

Boulder C

This rock forms the right side of the passageway.

❏ **45.** V4 A sweet SDS under the bulge requires good sloper technique and provides good value for being so short.

❏ **46.** V6 Reverse Traverse. Start low on the right and traverse left into Problem 7 to add a few stout moves.

❏ **47.** VB Big edges on a slab above a bush lead to a rounded topout.

The House Boulder

Check out a classic V4 and a project that's repelled all suitors. While only a hundred feet off the main trail, you can't see it hiding in the trees. To get there, head up the trail another fifty yards beyond the second entrance to the Crawford Boulders and look to your left. You should see a smallish boulder (it has a few short, mediocre problems) off in the trees.

Just ahead is a broken log crossing the trail, with a short cutoff piece right of the trail. Beyond that you'll see a thin, tapering log on the right. At the far end of this tapering log, on your left a super faint trail leads almost straight away from the trail – within one minute of leaving the trail you should see the boulder.

❏ **48. Burning Down The House** V4/5 This obvious bulging prow on your right as you walk up to the boulder is the best problem on this boulder and absolutely worth walking out here for.

❏ **49.** V? Project. This lurking impossibility has tiny crimps and huge moves, starting just left of a big, bent tree growing from under the boulder. Local legend says Sharma tried it and got shut down.

❏ **50.** V3 Good edges lead over a bulge just right of a boulder on the ground.

❏ **51.** V5 High start on small holds left of the boulder, out the left side of the overhang.

❏ **52.** V3 Another high start on smallish holds, with a hard SDS project leading into it. 8 feet left of Problem 3.

The slabby faces of this boulder have many possible warmup type variations.

Upper Old County

Once you've ticked the lower area, take a short hike and get ready for more great moves. There's a boulder just over the hill from here that doesn't have much, but another three minutes will get you a highball extravaganza. The lone boulder's got 26 problems on it, and if you go around the left corner of the low cliffband just uphill from it, you'll pass some lower quality rock and then come to a super cool overhang made up of distinctive horizontal plates with a bunch of great highballs on it.

Rope Boulder

This big, proud, tall boulder is the start of the upper area, with the highest concentration of good problems up here on solid rock. The problems here are numbered from the bottom of a prominent V-shaped feature on the back side.

❏ **1. V3** Serious due to a rock in the landing zone. SDS at a big edge below the right side of the V-feature and follow the crack through the bulge to a baffling top out.

❏ **2. Sit Down and Smoke This V8** Same start as Problem 1, but traverse along the seam to the right to decent edges and a massive throw to a small pocket. Athletic and technical.

❏ **3. Smoke This V5** Gotta be easier than 2. Stand start in the middle of 2 and finish on the throw.

❏ **4. V?** Start above a small bush with your left hand in an obvious slot and your right on a small sloper, then toss for the mossy crack.

❏ **5. VB** Low angle moves with good holds lead up left of a mossy streak.

❏ **6. V0** SDS to edge and slot just right of the mossy streak.

❏ **7. VB** Down route. Crack starting on rock to a left-trending ledge.

❏ **8. VB** Slab moves with great holds.

❏ **9. V0** Slab moves with great holds.

❏ **10. V3** SDS below a well-featured prow.

❏ **11. V0** Stand start 10 at a fantastic bucket hold. Eliminates the hard move but makes this a better warm-up.

❏ **12. V1** Start at 11 but half way along the traverse take off upwards on bomber edges.

❏ **13. V1** Either start on 11 and traverse in, or start low in the dihedral on the left side of the V-feature and head up the crack on good jams and holds.

❏ **14. V3** SDS at an undercling below the crack and finish on 13. One move adds two V-grades.

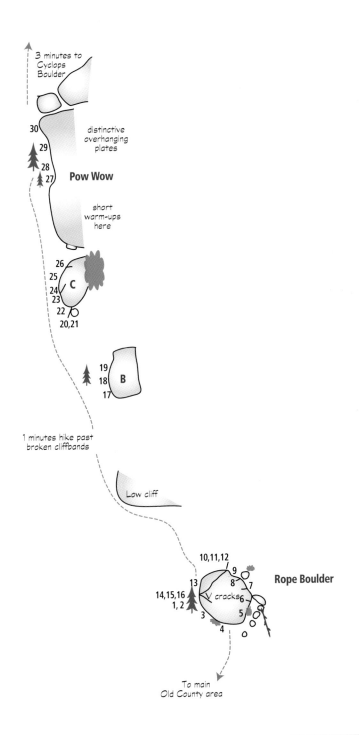

3 minutes to
Cyclops
Boulder

30

29

28

27

distinctive
overhanging
plates

Pow Wow

short
warm-ups
here

26

25

24

23

22

20,21

C

19

18

17

B

1 minutes hike past
broken cliffbands

Low cliff

10,11,12

9

8

7

13

Rope Boulder

14,15,16

1, 2

V cracks

6

3

5

4

To main
Old County area

❏ **15.** V3 SDS on 1 but finish on 14.

❏ **16.** V3 Same start, but finish straight up the prow between the cracks on good edges.

One minute's walk past some boulders and cliffbands that might harbor some potential there are three more outcroppings that have worthwhile problems on them.

Boulder B

This low, overhanging boulder has more features than you'll know what to do with, and a leaning flake on the right side. It's off to the right of the trail about 50 feet.

❏ **17.** V1 Good holds through an overhang on crazy, stacked horizontal flakes.

❏ **18.** V1 Low start to a dihedral in the center of the formation.

❏ **19.** V1 SDS to good holds on the left side of the bulge.

Boulder C

This tall, overhanging boulder right by the trail has some great problems on it. A couple lean toward highballs.

❏ **20.** V0 Start on gray rock with big holds just right of the overhanging prow, and traverse up and right on buckets.

❏ **21.** V2 This is great fun. Start as for 20, but finish directly up the bulge.

❏ **22. High-Speed Dirt** V6 Start on small holds under the lowest part of the overhang and slap your way up on small edges and sidepulls.

❏ **23. Dirt Torpedo** V5 Claw at small, painful edges between the left side of the bulge and the crack. Feels steeper than it looks.

❏ **24.** V0 Follow the obvious crack for a few cool moves.

❏ **25.** V0 Well-featured rock just left of the crack can be a separate line if you don't use the crack.

❏ **26.** V0 SDS to a short crack problem.

Pow Wow

Next up is the Pow Wow Boulder, a long cliffband with a proud overhang on the uphill end of it. It's composed of obvious, striking horizontals like a cabinet full of dishes.

❏ **27.** V3 Right side of the roof, starting at a color change in the rock behind the big tree.

❏ **28.** V1 Start in the center of the formation, and head up and right on positive holds to a difficult roof sequence. This loose variation is a little high and hollow.

❏ **29.** V1 Tall, fantastic problem with great moves. Some of the plates seem kinda funky, but they're probably solid for now.

❏ **30.** V2 Shorty problem on good holds under the low roof. Worth doing as long as you're up here anyway.

The Cyclops Boulder

The Cyclops Boulder is three minutes uphill from the Pow Wow Boulder and has three decent problems on it, plus a big pocket in the center (thus the name).

❏ **1. Cyclops V2** Start low on the right side of the boulder, work your way up and left through the eye and top out a little higher than is comfortable.

❏ **2. V2** Same start, but finish up and right. Not as tall, not as good.

❏ **3. V3** Straight up left of the eye is worth doing, and a little harder.

The Future Boulders

Aptly named, these are the future of Old County for now. Situated a five-minute bushwhack above the Cyclops Boulder on a deer trail, the Futures harbor good potential over spooky landings on fantastic rock. Various local climbers have poked around up here and some of what you see has been done, but the harder stuff is still waiting. If you've ticked everything lower on the hill, come up here and get served. One problem worth mentioning is a problem about 100 yards uphill and slightly east from Cyclops, called Stinkin, Drinkin, Never Thinkin, roughly V5.

Continuing above and left of the Futures along the ridgeline might yield more potential, and there's certainly more lurking in the woods around here. While investigating is always painful and seldom fruitful, sometimes you get lucky and stumble on the next big thing. Don't be afraid to bring your Carharrts and get after it...

The Binder

Approach time: **20 minutes**

Season: **April-November**

Number of problems: **37**

The Binder has a number of high and mostly moderate problems. This is some of the best rock in the Old County area. However, due to the tall nature of the problems, and the 15 minutes of extra hiking, The Binder sees few crowds. The landings are flat and you get a great view of Lake Tahoe. The harder problems go into the shade in the afternoon.

Problem 29.

Driving Directions

Follow the same driving directions to Old County.

Approach

Follow the approach to the main Old County area (the Crawford Boulder, etc). Instead of turning off the main road, continue for five minutes until you get to a fork in the road. Take the right fork and continue for another five minutes. Keep an eye out for a forked tree with a small boulder next to it on the left of the road. From here, follow a faint trail on the right side of road which turns into an barely discernable old road. Follow the road uphill toward the ridge for about ten minutes until you arrive at The Binder.

Bloodsucker Boulder

Freestanding boulder with many enjoyable problems. Almost good for beginners: high but slabs off on one side.

❏ **1. VB** Right-leaning crack on slab.

❏ **2. VB** Arête.

❏ **3. V0** Pockets just right of arête.

❏ **4. VB** Pockets on slab.

❏ **5. VB** Pockets on slab.

❏ **6. V0** Arête above detached flake.

❏ **7. V1** Flake system to edges.

❏ **8. V1** Another flake system.

❏ **9. VB** Arête.

❏ **10. V0** Overhanging crack with buckets.

Number of problems by difficulty

VB	V0	V1	V2	V3	V4	V5	V6	V7	V8	V9	V10	≥V11
9	7	8	1	2	3	1	1					

SUPERTOPO

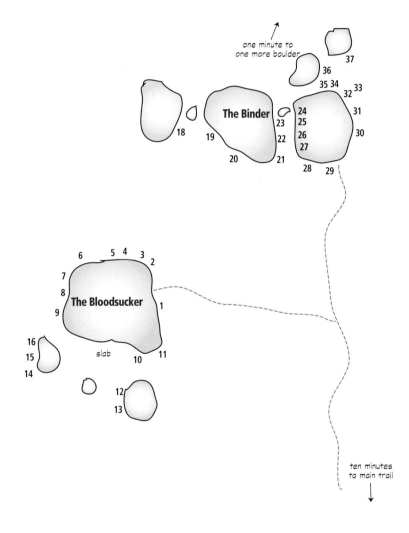

one minute to
one more boulder

37

36
35 34   33
          32   33
                    31

The Binder   24
              23 25
              22 26
                  27
18   19   21
    20   28   29

6   5 4 3
              2
7
8   The Bloodsucker   1
9
16
15   slab   10 11
14   10

12
13

17

ten minutes
to main trail

❏ **11. V2** SDS on short overhanging section.

❏ **12. V0** Crack on the middle of face.

❏ **13. V0** Face moves to arête.

❏ **14. V3** Mossy arête.

❏ **15. V4** Thin, short face.

❏ **16. V3** Shorter thin face.

❏ **17. V1** Undercling over roof on self side of boulder.

The Binder

Warm up on the tall easier problems, then head over to Problems 30-34.

❏ **18. V1** Turn a small roof. Super high.

❏ **19. VB** Left-side face.

❏ **20. V1** Middle of face.

❏ **21. VB** Tall. Right of arête.

❏ **22. V0** Six feet right of arête.

❏ **23. V0** Right-side face.

❏ **24. V1** Start left of rock.

❏ **25. V1** Start off rock.

❏ **26. V1** Over green lichen.

❏ **27. V0** Just left of arête.

❏ **28. V0** Right of arête.

❏ **29. V0** Just right of center.

❏ **30. V4 Day of Reckoning** Main line up steep face.

❏ **31. V5 Last Judgement** Blackish rock. Big move to big pocket.

❏ **32. V6 Basking in Glory** Proud arête. SDS is likely V8.

❏ **33. V8 Swimming in Shit** V8 start left and traverse into Basking in Glory.

❏ **34. V4 Moffititis** Right of arête. Pockets over bulge.

❏ **35. V8 Pintar** This might be the SDS of Moffititis.

❏ **36. V6 Chasing the Dragon** Or maybe this is the SDS to Moffititis.

❏ **37. VB**

❏ **38. VB**

White Lines

Approach time: **2 minutes**

Season: **May-November**

Number of problems: **5**

Situated a short boulder hop downhill from the road cut parking lot on Donner Summit is a cluster of boulders with a few good problems on them, all of which are hard and incredible. They're also either on or near private property, and accessing them from the dirt road is a great way to cause trouble in the future. While talus-skiing isn't that much fun, it's also not far enough to justify losing access to this granite trove.

Driving Directions

From the north side of Donner Lake, at the junction of Donner Lake Road and Donner Pass Road, drive 1.9 miles west and park at the dirt pullout on the left. Jump the guardrail and scramble down a few hundred feet of talus.

From the Snowshed Wall (wall just east of the arched stone bridge), drive 0.9 miles and park on a dirt pullout on the left. Jump the guardrail and scramble down a few hundred feet of talus.

❑ **1. White Lines V8** White Lines has all the classic elements– steep rock, big moves, and a scary topout, all situated on an obvious, proud line. At V8, this problem has been called "Tahoe's Midnight Lightning," and while I'm wary of such comparisons, in this case it's apt. Steal the beta from Wills Young's film titled, "Lisa Rands." Yep, it's her, pulling down.

❑ **2. Pimp Slap V9** To the right of White Lines, this climbs the slopers up into the upper crux of White Lines.

❑ **3. The Short Bus Arête V4** The clean arête that faces the White Lines boulder.

❑ **4. The School Bus Traverse V6** To the left of The Short Bus Arête, start down low and traverse the sloping lip up right.

❑ **5. The Real Deal V10** The Real Deal is just that. Another wicked, horizontal problem that checks in around V10 and has seen very few ascents is lurking one minute downhill of the White Lines boulder. From the top of White Lines you can see it, or just follow a faint trail through the brush from the downhill side of White Lines you'll come around the right side of The Real Deal and see the only line there. Get some!

The other big blocks have futuristic projects and some topropes on them.

Kiss My Aspen Boulder

One mile east of the Snowshed Wall (0.1 miles east of White Lines) is a boulder about 10 feet above the road. It is a good warm up spot before going to White Lines. Park in the big dirt/paved pullout on the east side of the road. The first problem you come to is a project six feet left of an aspen tree. Big moves on diagonal cracks. The next problem is Kiss My Aspen (V2). It climbs the right side of the face next to an aspen tree. On the west side of the boulder is Grease Lightning (V2/V3). Low start on a rail. Dyno up and left.

Number of problems by difficulty

VB	V0	V1	V2	V3	V4	V5	V6	V7	V8	V9	V10	≥V11
0	0	0	0	0	1	0	1	1	1	1	0	0

Tommy Caldwell on White Lines. Photo by Corey Rich.

Sun Wall

Approach time: **2 minute**

Season: **April-November**

Number of problems: **25**

Sunset on the Sun Wall.

Aptly named, the Sun Wall bouldering area is good anytime the weather isn't horrible. You can slog up through the snow, take off your winter gear, and climb in a T-shirt in January. Nice. Most of the problems are V1-V3 with flat landings. This wall also has some of the best highballs and solos around. They're huge and terrifying, but not that hard. Which can be kind of a problem, actually, since getting suckered into doing one of these babies is that much easier. Whatever you decide, don't do it just for photos or props. If you fall off you'll drop 30 feet, bounce once and drop another 20 feet on the way into traffic. A pad will do you no good at all.

Sunny southern exposure means the Sun Wall boulders are climbable yearround, but in the winter you will have to walk through tons of snow to get to them.

Driving Directions

From Truckee, drive up Donner Lake Road past the arched bridge after Snowshed Wall, and park on either side of the road at your first possible opportunity. If you're coming from Sacramento, take the Soda Springs exit and head straight past the hotel/bar on your left. You'll come down Donner Lake Road until you can see the arched bridge ahead, and park just before it.

Approach

The problems are right above the road. Just hike 50-100 feet up the hill on a faint trail through broken, stepped terrain.

Number of problems by difficulty

VB	V0	V1	V2	V3	V4	V5	V6	V7	V8	V9	V10	≥V11
1	1	3	10	5	3	1	0	0	0	0	0	0

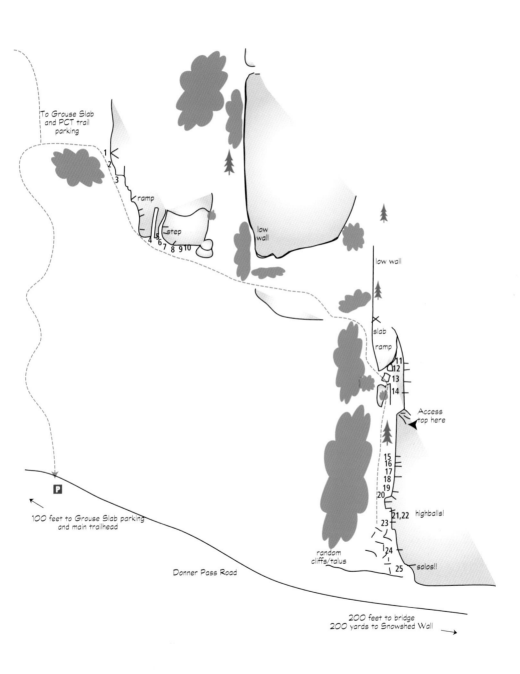

Sun Wall

Problems are numbered starting at the trail coming in from Grouse Slabs down to the road, and it's worth doing them in that order to be sure you're warm for the big 'uns.

❏ **1. VB** Fingers to hands crack. Good moves, if a little low angle.

❏ **2. V2** Start up the crack, but then move right to the arête for a stouter finish to 1.

❏ **3. V3** A powerful start on the arête proper (rock to the right is off) makes this even more fun. SDS is around V4ish.

❏ **4. V2** Climb the cracks. Crunchy and not that fun.

❏ **5. V4** Arête, SDS using the diagonal crack on the left side of the arête, then finish out right.

❏ **6. V2** Work your way up the prow on the right side.

❏ **7. V1** Follows some face features six feet left of the groove.

❏ **8. V2** Great face climbing on small features in the groove by the seam.

❏ **9. V4** Tiny holds just right of the seam will test your skin.

❏ **10. V2** Slab climbing four feet right of the subtle bulge.

❏ **11. V0** Climb the left of the twin cracks.

❏ **12. V3** Climb the right crack to a spicy, interesting finish.

❏ **13. Project V?** Looks desperate, some holds might fall off, but you won't want to because the landing's not great.

❏ **14. V3** A right facing sidepull starts this problem, at the bottom of the last crack before the break that accesses the top of the highballs.

❏ **15. V4** Sidepull and swing between these parallel cracks, starting at the bottom left and ending at the top right.

❏ **16. V3** Start at the bottom of the second crack from the tree, sidepulling the third crack to the same finish as 15.

❏ **17. V5** The face between the cracks. There's not much to work with here.

❏ **18. V2** Flaring crack start just right of step down in the path. Feels tall.

❏ **19. V1** Twin cracks in the dihedral. Bomber jams and solid holds still manage to seem small towards the top.

❏ **20. V1** It starts getting real right about here. The first crack right of the dihedral is guarded by a bad landing that would require many pads to improve. Better not to test it.

❏ **21. V2** Start in the right-facing dihedral, then undercling the obvious overlap out left and finish on 20. Harder and just as tall.

❏ **22. V2** Take the crack/dihedral line up and right.

❏ **23. V2** Start right of the dihedral, then take a slopey rail up and left into the dihedral at half height.

❏ **24. V3** Okay, we're not bouldering anymore. These last two are solos. A flaring finger crack leads into thin twin cracks. It's hard, scary, and insecure so you want to be absolutely rock solid at this grade.

❏ **25. V2** The right-facing dihedral has a steep start and is the last crack accessible from this side of things. A must-do for any aspiring mind-control expert.

Grouse Slabs

Approach time: **10 minutes**

Season: **May-November**

Number of problem: **55**

The views from here are pretty impressive so bring your camera and some sponsor-hungry friends and make some magic. If you get any swag, send some my way. First thing in the morning on a fall day the conditions are absolutely perfect. You'll want a thermos of espresso and your puffy jacket, but all the holds will feel a half size bigger. In the summer forget climbing here during the day. Poach somebody's pier and take a swim down at the lake.

Driving Directions

Follow the same driving directions as for the Sun Wall and park in roughly the same spot.

Approach

The Pacific Crest Trail hits the road here on the right side up by Bastille Slab, the obvious practice area right down by the road. Pick up the Pacific Crest Trail on the right, and follow it perpendicular to the road as it winds past two cut logs and a couple of ponds on your left. Just as you come out of the woods, stop for a second and look around. You'll see a giant dead tree on the hillside opposite you, with boulders scattered around it for a hundred yards in any direction. The best and largest boulders are to the right and behind the snag, while the ones in the foreground are smaller and poorly defined. Now that you're oriented, the bunch of social trails running every which way won't be so confusing. There's one more boulder out here that's easy to miss. It's down and to your right in the ravine between where you come out of the woods and where the main boulders are, and it's got a few problems on it (not shown).

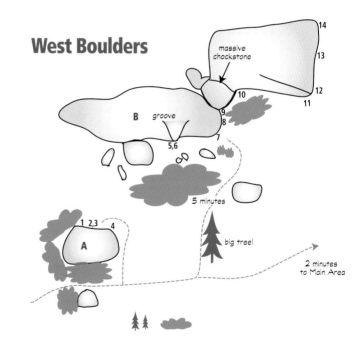

West Boulders

Number of problems by difficulty

VB	V0	V1	V2	V3	V4	V5	V6	V7	V8	V9	V10	≥V11
8	5	7	11	6	4	2	1	1	0	0	0	0

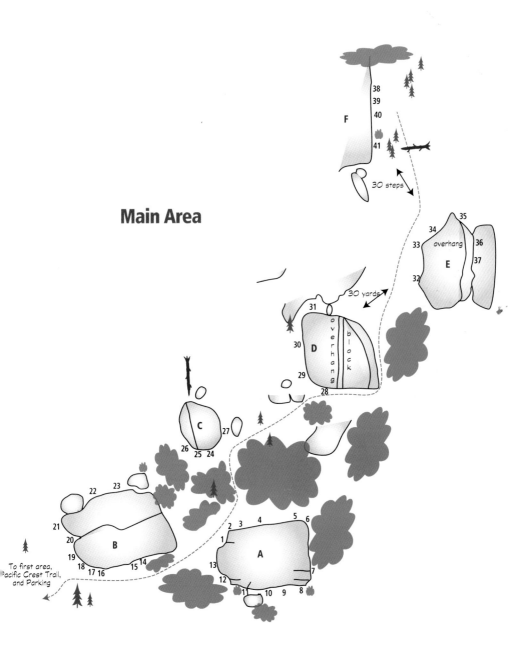

Main Area

Boulder A

The first boulder you can get to in front of all the others has a couple of short problems on the back side facing uphill.

❏ **1. V0** Right-side face, two moves.

❏ **2. V5** Contrived SDS right of 3. Hardly worth it.

❏ **3. V2** SDS up to the point.

❏ **4. V2** SDS on left side of face, traverse into end of 2.

Boulder B

There's a cluster of giant blocks about 150 feet uphill from the little boulder with some worthwhile endeavors on them.

❏ **5. V5** SDS on right-facing sidepull and crank over the lip.

❏ **6. V8/9** Start on 5, but traverse the entire lip out and right on slopers, campusing madly and pawing for footholds. Good luck.

❏ **7. Project V?** Another ridiculous challenge. Try to haul yourself off the ground on this overhanging arête. If you can manage that, the rest will probably go.

❏ **8. V2** Tallish, Tuolumne-style knob pimping fun.

❏ **9. VB** Follow the holds around the crack.

❏ **10. V3** Small, insecure holds. Delicate footwork is needed.

❏ **11. V2** Great crack moves lead to a stressful ending. The landing starts to get bad just as the holds do, too.

❏ **12. V3** Right side arête.

❏ **13. V0-V2** Many good slab variations are possible here.

❏ **14. VB** Arête at the uphill end of the slab.

If you walk around the base of the hill with the dead snag on it, headed for Grouse Slabs, you'll find these boulders perched on the flats just where the view gets really good. The two in the foreground have the highest concentration of great problems.

Boulder A

The big boulder with the dihedral is described first.

❏ **1. V0** Lieback and stem the dihedral/thin crack. Check out the cool white dike on your way by.

❏ **2. V1** Arête left of the dihedral.

❏ **3. V4** SDS on a profusion of small, bad holds. This is frustrating, especially if your tips are sore.

❏ **4. V2** Start on the obvious rail. Cool sequence.

❏ **5. V1** Low start just right of the arête.

❏ **6. VB** Left side of the arête.

❏ **7. VB** Twin cracks on the corner.

❏ **8. V0** Start just to the left of the corner. It gets harder the farther left you go.

❏ **9. V3** Hard slab moves just right of the big taco chip.

❏ **10. V0** Crank up the right side of the taco chip to the slab.

❏ **11. VB** Follow the low-angle crack on the prow.

❏ **12. VB** Discontinuous cracks right of the slabby face.

❏ **13. VB** Slabby Y-shaped crack just right of the dihedral.

Boulder B

❏ **14. V2** Delicate face climbing on small crimps. Tricky in the middle.

❏ **15. V3** Start on 14, but traverse the small crack way out left and finish at the crack in the notch.

❏ **16. Project V?** There's probably a direct start to 15, on miserable holds.

❏ **17. V6** Traverse small edges to the left, feet swinging wildly, to finish on 19.

❏ **18. Project V?** From the deepest pocket in the middle of 17, slap vainly for a tiny edge up high.

❏ **19. V4** SDS. A good time. Get down and dirty, then haul yourself up the overhang. Thuggish and shouldery, it doesn't end out left. Go straight up for full value.

❏ **20. Project V?** V-God knows. Ghastly lie-down start to a seven-foot roof chimney. Do this, and everybody buys your drinks tonight.

❏ **21. V7** Short slappy problem on bad slopers.

❏ **22. V3** Great traverse on crack to a dyno that's bigger than it looks. It's hard to keep your butt off the boulder at the beginning.

❏ **23. V2** Grab the best hold at the end of the crack and pop for the jug above.

Boulder C

This boulder has a white dike running all the way through it, and a friend of mine from Vermont called it a wishing stone. The deal is, if a rock has a different color stripe that goes all the way through it then you can wish on it, but only once. Make it a good one.

❏ **24. V1** The right side of the downhill face.

❏ **25. VB** Follow the white stripe.

❏ **26. V2** SDS at a knob and a sloper on the gold patina face.

❏ **27. V1** Start on the low horizontal and go over the bugle.

Boulder D

This boulder is distinctive. It's got a huge chunk that fell off the far side and made a totally square-cut overhanging section. The near side has a big tree growing next to it.

❏ **28. V3** One big move on great holds.

❏ **29. V1** Jump start this if you're short. Three-move wonder just right of the tree.

❏ **30. V1** Slab, first move is the crux.

❏ **31. V2** Hard first move at the right end of the overhang, up into the dihedral.

Boulder E

The boulder right in front of Grouse Slab is just like D. The same kind of block fell off, forming the same kind of overhang facing the same direction.

❏ **32. V?** SDS under a sharp, overhanging arête on small holds.

❏ **33. V1** Big hold with bad feet on the rounded arête.

❏ **34. V3** Grim slab moves on tiny holds.

❏ **35. V5** Fantastic problem with strange body positioning and moves. Start just left of the arête and finish around the right side on slopers.

❏ **36. V2** This problem appears to dead-end at the roof.

❏ **37. V4** This massive, horizontal throw goes out the roof off bad slopers, and looks hard. Watch the landing, too.

❏ **38. V1** Sloping holds to micro-edging just left of the bushes.

❏ **39. V1** Tiny holds on the slab right of the crack.

❏ **40. V0** Crack in the center of the slab. Cool moves on good jams.

❏ **41. V1** Micro-tiny holds make this strange, balancey problem kind of painful.

Boulder F

There's a small subsidiary slab right under Grouse that's got a few decent problems on it, all of them low angle.

Misc. Donner Summit

School House Rock

From just west of the scenic Donner bridge, drive 200 feet and at the base of a slab. A fifty-foot trail links the road to the Pacific Crest Trail (PCT). At the top of this trail, up the right side of the Kindergarten Rock, is a prime nugget along the PCT. The right/west side has a sweet straight-up wall with thin edges that turns the corner on the left. There are also straight-up and right side variations. The leftside facing the road has a very nice sit start to an overhanging crack. There is a harder problem right with an SDS.

Going west a few feet on the PCT, there is a boulder with no bottom. A few feet farther up the PCT is a sit start (ass on the PCT) with feet back in a small cave, that goes up some small edges. Very Hard.

Continue up the PCT past the top of Kindergarten Rock. At the bottom of the Kindergarten cracks is a boulder on the PCT with a steep face (facing west) that has a hollow flake on it. One problem starts on the far right and moves left around the corner and ends with a top out on the point. The left problem starts on the hollow flake, slaps the top and finished to the right on the point. There are number of problems in the boulders behind this one, but none worthy singling out. There are also some good moderate problems around the base of Kindergarten Cracks including the Blackboard. There are also a number of problems on top of and around the sides of School House Rock including a couple of highball cracks about halfway up the east face of school house that start at a grassy bench (five star cracks 5.10-5.11). Lots of rock around School House for those looking for a little adventure and some good climbs. Back east on the PCT, under the sport climb Short Subject, there is a nugget that has some good steep problems that have probably become overgrown in recent years.

Garbage Pail Traverse

To get to this five-star problem, walk west on the PCT to the gully that descends from the top of School House Rock. Toward the top of the gully is a bulging overhang of compact granite. The problem starts low on the left and traverses up and right around the bulge. There are at least three variations.

Baboon Crag Traverse

This high quality problem traverses the overhang under the routes at Baboon Crag. It is located at the top of Old Highway 40 right across the street from the ASI/Sugar Bowl Academy House. Follow the PCT north for about 30 yards and the routes (few bolts)/traverse are right next to the trail. Steep and high quality. Very hard to actually link it up. Bunch of moderate bouldering around the base of Baboon Crag. This area is normally windy, so an excellent place to go if the mosquitoes are bad on the summit.

Donner Peak

There are numerous high quality problems on the various outcrops on and around the summit of Donner Peak including the mega-classic Football Field Traverse. It features over 50 yards of steep face and flakes moving up and left. It is located in the gash that splits the summit. It faces north and can be seen from the Old Highway 40. The first section is very hard with a bad landing, but the remainder climbs like a 5.11 route but never to far off the ground. The rock is excellent and unique. It is also a nice place to get away from the crowds. There are many faces and overhangs. Don't miss the outcrops a few hundred feet down from the summit on the west side. There are about 50 high quality problems including some excellent overhands. Definitely worth the hike (30-45 minutes). To get here, follow the Pacific Crest Trail south from the trail head near the summit of Old Highway 40. Walk about a mile down the Lake Mary Road to a junction in the trail located in the middle of one of the ski runs that heads back to the summit of Donner Peak.

Black Wall

There is a V10 on the approach to the south side of the Black Wall. The problem climbs the steep underside of a boulder about half-way up the approach.

Top of Snowshed

Approach time: **2 minutes**

Season: **May-November**

Number of problems: **34**

Sweet granite bouldering in a great setting with a tiny approach—does it get any better? You'll love this stuff. When it's a zillion degrees down lower, it will still be nice up here, with the wind and thermals keeping things cool. The only downside is weekends, when the entire pass looks like an anthill that just got poked with a stick. If you're bouldering here, don't forget to tell everybody that there's a lot more to be had in the Tahoe basin besides just Donner.

Please be super careful when bouldering up here, as Snowshed Wall is the most popular area around. If you kick something off, it's going to hit somebody. If it's something big, it's going to kill them. Also, there are some tempting-looking problems along the edges of Boulders A and C above the gullies, but be aware that these are not boulder problems. They're solos, the highest highballs you'll ever do, with the whole of Snowshed Wall lurking below if you pitch off or stumble over the edge.

Kevin Swift on Problem 5, (V2).

From the Snowshed Wall parking lot, hike up to the Snowshed Wall then skirt the base right to a sandy gully that tunnels under a huge chockstone. This chockstone is Boulder A.

Driving Directions

From Truckee, drive up Donner Lake Road and park in front of the Snowshed Wall (the big obvious wall on your left a few hundred feet before the arched stone bridge).

If you're coming from Sacramento or the Bay Area, take Interstate 80 to the Soda Springs exit. Take Donner Pass Road just past the arched bridge and park on the right in front of the Snowshed Wall.

Number of problems by difficulty

VB	V0	V1	V2	V3	V4	V5	V6	V7	V8	V9	V10	≥V11
3	2	2	4	3	3	0	2	2	3	0	0	0

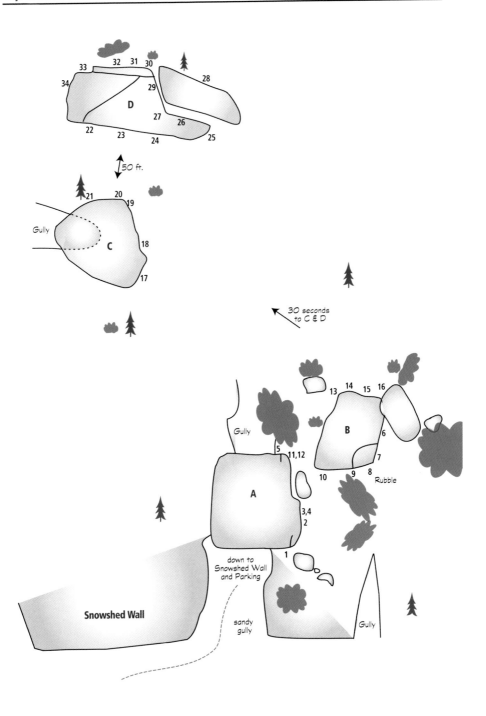

Boulder A

This is a huge chockstone straddling a gully, and has great problems on it.

❏ **1.** V2 Lieback the crack on the left side of this arête.

❏ **2. Project** V? Go up and left from the middle of 3.

❏ **3.** V6 Stellar problem on good, obvious edges. Starts with big move up and left.

❏ **4.** V8 Same start, go up and right on tiny, painful crimps. So far it's only had one ascent.

❏ **5.** V2 Good moves up a seam.

Boulder B

The shorter boulder across from A.

❏ **6.** V? Traverse the face at mid-height.

❏ **7.** V? Up the problem on right side of the arête on small holds.

❏ **8.** VB The arête.

❏ **9.** VB Great low-angle handcrack. Get training.

❏ **10.** VB Slab problem.

❏ **11.** V0 Go up big holds to a flat, slopey topout.

❏ **12.** V3 Start on 6, traverse left, and finish on Problem 8. Sweet sequences.

❏ **13. V3** Start at the sloping hold on the arête and finish up and left.

❏ **14. V7/8** SDS to bad, small holds and a sidepull.

❏ **15. V4** Crack problem.

❏ **16. V?** One move dyno off slopes.

Boulder C

This is another chockstone, with a huge overhang facing towards the gully that drops down to Snowshed.

❏ **17. V0** Slabby.

❏ **18. V2** Licheny dihedral.

❏ **19. V3** One-move mantel on flakes.

❏ **20. Project V?** Pinch and slap your way up the arête.

❏ **21. Project V?** Possible hard moves on a left-trending seam.

Boulder D

Big boulder with it's tallest face downhill towards Boulder C.

❏ **22. V7** Hard moves on small crimps on the left side of the face. Featured in the movie Rampage with Chris Sharma throwing down.

❏ **23. Project** Even harder moves on bad crimps in the middle of the face.

❏ **24. V8** Start with your right hand in a little pod and left on a crimp, suck it up and go. Mega-classic if you crank this hard.

❏ **25. V6** Sick, steep crack moves under a narrow roof.

❏ **26. V1** Slab moves in the corridor.

❏ **27. V2** Stem the dihedral.

❏ **28. Project V?** SDS on small holds seven feet left of the tree.

❏ **29. V?** Steep moves on good holds above a slab landing.

❏ **30. V1** Traverse the long horizontal crack.

❏ **31. V?** Exit Problem 30 at a right-facing feature near the left end.

❏ **32. V?** Exit Problem 30 at features under bright yellow-green lichen.

❏ **33. V?** Yeah, good luck. SDS at the back of a low roof—pull endless roof crack moves to the lip.

❏ **34. V4** Traverse the lip of a low overhang around into the end of 12.

Some minor potential exists on the blocks uphill from D but not much.

The Saddle

Approach time: **1 minute**

Season: **June-November**

Number of problems: **40+**

The Saddle boulders have the highest concentration of hard problems in the Tahoe basin. The rock quality is superb and every problem is worth doing. Come here if you're hard core and you won't regret it. There are also some great moderate problems. You have to earn the remote ambiance with a fairly involved drive.

Driving Directions

The approach is interesting—you have to drive through a mile of old train tunnels. The tracks have been pulled up, but the tunnels remain, and they've even got a bunch of windows looking out over Donner Summit and Donner Lake. The only downside is if someone's coming the other direction, there's generally no room to pass so one of you will have to back up. I'm not sure what the local protocol on this one. Maybe rock-paper-scissors and the loser backs up?

Drive Interstate 80 to Soda Springs Road exit, which intersects Donner Summit Road. Drive a few miles until you start running into ski resort paraphernalia. You're looking for Donner Ski Ranch, the resort on the left. Across the road, you'll see a big industrial-looking gravel parking lot, with the tunnel opening in the hillside (the Sugarbowl access road passees right over the tunnel entrance). Drive 3.5 miles through the three or so tunnels and then on a road with unusually deep gravel that's good fun for practicing your rally driving skills.

There are two dirt roads that take off on the uphill side of the gravel road. You want

the second one. It runs uphill about 50 yards and then there's a parking lot on the left side big enough for five or six cars. The boulders are on the right side of the road as you drive in, and you can see the warm up boulder from the parking lot. The Saddle Boulder proper is downhill a bit from the Black Wall and warmup boulder.

NOTE: Occasionally, the train tunnels close. In that case you will need a 4 x 4. Follow the directions for getting to Split Rock. Start at the junction of the road leaving the state park and the road that passes the gravel pits (sometimes the gate on Coldstream Road, just past the Holiday Inn, is locked). Head out into Coldstream Canyon from this junction; at 0.8 miles, take the left junction, passing the ponds; at 1.7 miles bear left, heading up the valley; at 3.1 miles, where the road meets the railroad

Number of problems by difficulty

VB	V0	V1	V2	V3	V4	V5	V6	V7	V8	V9	V10	≥V11
2	3	0	2	6	4	2	2	1	2	2	2	1

tracks, bear left; at 3.3 miles, head through the tunnel (the "mouse hole"), heading right after leaving the tunnel; at 3.7 miles, bear right, following the sign towards "n. fork cold creek"; at 5.5 miles, bear right; at 6.4 miles will be the parking for The Saddle. There are numerous spur roads off of this one that must be avoided, but most are obvious that you don't want to take them. Be aware the tunnel contains a seasonally

raging stream so this option may not work in the earlier part of the summer.

At 5.0 miles, park in a small clearing and walk straight into the woods for a few minutes. You'll find a large boulder with ~10 problems, V0-V8(?). Definitely worth checking out

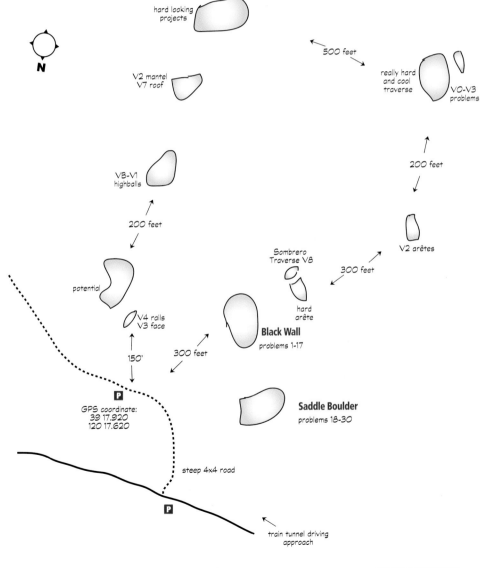

hard looking projects

500 feet

N

V2 mantel
V7 roof

really hard
and cool
traverse

V0-V3
problems

200 feet

V3-V1
highballs

V2 arêtes

200 feet

Sombrero
Traverse V8

300 feet

potential

hard
arête

V4 rails
V3 face

Black Wall
problems 1-17

150'

300 feet

P
GPS coordinate:
39 17.920
120 17.620

Saddle Boulder
problems 18-30

steep 4x4 road

P

train tunnel driving
approach

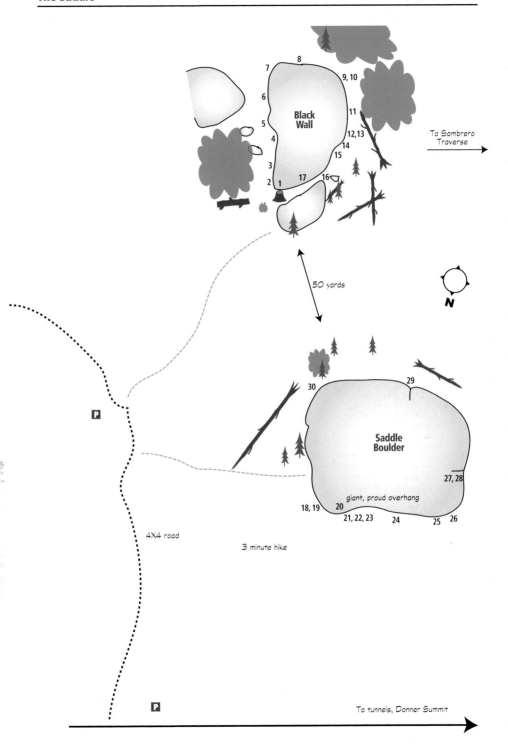

Black Wall

❏ **1. Mars Belly V4** Start on top of the stump at a huge hold and dyno up and right to a bucket.

❏ **2. V3** SDS left of the stump and go straight up the prow. There's something that might go up and left from here also.

❏ **3. Nazgul V9** Stand start on a pile of cheater stones in front of "PAM" graffiti. Crimp the seam and go to small pockets and edges. It's probably V11 if you do the proper start with two hands on the undercling. V10 if you start with one hand on the undercling.

❏ **4. V6** Start in the mini-dihedral and follow rounded sidepulls and pinches.

❏ **5. V3** Low angle. Start at two slopey pockets and head up the slab.

❏ **6. V3** Another slab. Start at two more pockets above the inverted "T" graffiti.

❏ **7. V0** Pull out the right side of a tiny roof to the slab above.

❏ **8. Kito Slab V5** Horridly frustrating slab. It's great.

❏ **9. V2** Low start below a small dihedral/

roof leads right into the crack.

❏ **10. Spirit Slips Away V6** Same start, but go straight up steep rock on good holds left of the crack.

❏ **11. V2** SDS at a sloper leads into edges and a seam.

❏ **12. V4** SDS at a big, low shelf, dyno up and finish off with a mantel.

❏ **13. V2** SDS on opposing pinches and climb straight up into scoop.

❏ **14. V0** Fantastic warmup. Follow the crack and jugs up and left, then reverse the problem, then run a few more laps just for fun. It's good for you.

There is a great V3 traverse that starts on Problem 9 and finishes on Problem 14.

❏ **15. Rosey Palms V5** Strange, awkward palm/ stem sequence in the scoop below 14 leads to a mantel. If you can stick the first move, you're there.

❏ **16. V3** This problem is hiding in plain sight. Below the horizontal

dihedral that starts at Problem 1, there's a big chunk of rock that fell off. At the right hand end of this rock there are two low crimps that lead right to a rail and a sloper.

❏ **17. V2** Also obscure. Jump to the lip from a small, hidden undercling inside the horizontal dihedral near the midpoint.

If you stand with your back to Problem 5, you can see another boulder about 50 feet away. This has three problems on it: a warm-up facing you, a sick project on the right side, and the V7 Sombrero Traverse, which travels all the way around the lip of the boulder from low left to high right. Good fun.

The Saddle Boulder

❏ **18. V3** Traverse left under the tree and top out just right of the broken-off tree hugging the rock.

❏ **19. V4** Start at a sloper just right of the tree and mantel into the vague corner system.

❏ **20. V8** Huge! Either jump-start or traverse in from Midnight Train to an obvious rail, and fire for the sloper so very far above.

❏ **21. Midnight Train V7** The obvious edges at chest height lead straight up to a break in the lip and then traverse left.

❏ **22. Hobo V8** Same start, but traverse up and right to a taller finish in the center of the wall.

❏ **23. Wicks Problem V11** A low start on a right-handed undercling six feet right of Hobo leads to the same finish.

❏ **24. Soul Train V10** SDS on very low holds, a right-hand crimp and left-hand slope, and finish on Hobo.

❏ **25. Nietzsche Girls V9** Start on the right-hand arête of this wall at two sloping holds along a seam at chest height and finish straight up. The sit-start is V10 at a sloping rail down and left from the stand-start.

❏ **26. Nietzsche Boys V10** SDS on Nietzsche Girls, but finish on Hobo.

❏ **27. VB** Crack on the slab around the corner to the right of all this hard madness.

❏ **28. V0** Traverse right on the seam from the same start.

❏ **29. VB** Serious. Follow the crack in the left-facing dihedral. Don't warm up on this one, you want to have your head together first.

❏ **30. V4 Stop Dragging My Heart Around** Traverse from the middle of the east face all the way around the middle of the south face.

The Party Boulder

From the Saddle Boulder parking, drive another 0.3 miles to great camping and a cool boulder with about eight problems right next to the road. Most of the problems are VB-V1 with a few V3 and harder.

Split Rock

Approach time: **5 minutes**

Season: **April-Novembber**

Number of problems: **28**

This place has got some history to it for sure. People have been bouldering here since the beginning (well, almost) and it's easy to see why. Great problems on solid granite with a ten minute approach. There's even a swimming hole so close you could hobble there in your climbing shoes and plunge your scorched feet in the water. I say this because the first time I bouldered here it was in full sun, in June, and I had to wear my girlfriend's shoes because mine had blown out. Now, she's got some big feet, but they're not nearly big enough. The pain was spectacular and I nearly whipped off the slabs in the corridor because properly weighting my feet was impossible. You're not that dumb, though, so have a good time while you're here. Just remember to come early or late if it's summer.

Driving Directions

On the west end of Truckee, off Interstate 80, take Donner Lake Road. Just next to the freeway, you'll come to a couple of gas stations. The road that runs between them will take you toward the boulders, but you'll encounter a gate before too long.

The gate's a little strange. The Parks and Recreation folks try to keep the gate locked on the weekends, to be sure that vacationers who want to access the canyon have to drive through Donner Lake State Park and pay a day-use fee. Some of the locals who live up that way are less than psyched about having to futz with the gate every time they go home, and so leave it open. If you come in past the gate when it's open, somebody might close it behind you. Then you've gotta go up canyon a bit, turn around and exit through the park, possibly incurring a fee. So, better to park outside the gate and walk the extra 100 yards.

Approach

Walk up the road to the grungy parking lot where the road turns to gravel, then take a right on a trail that runs between the pond on your left and the campground on the right. You'll walk right up to it. Problems are numbered starting on the left arête of the first half of the boulder you come to. For the near side, downclimb #14. For the far side, Problem 26.

Number of problems by difficulty

VB	V0	V1	V2	V3	V4	V5	V6	V7	V8	V9	V10	≥V11
5	1	7	4	12	2	2	1	0	0	1	0	1

Split Rock, Near Half

This is the half you'll first walk up to.

❏ **1.** V3 Rounded arête, difficult start due to bad feet.

❏ **2.** V2 Direct start to 1 on good small edges.

❏ **3.** V5 Crimps through lichen to one gold edge to a sporty topout.

❏ **3a.** V9? Start on the big rail, go straight up to a diagonal gold edge and then trend slightly right to a right-facing shallow seam. V9? Or, go left to sloping gold dike.

❏ **4.** V6 SDS on a right-trending rail to a big dyno and a strange, convoluted topout. Good problem with a stopper move in the middle.

❏ **5. The Moffat Problem** V8 Looks wicked hard. Stand start in scoop on tiny crimps left of the right-hand arête.

❏ **6. Bear Hug Arête** V4 Up the rounded arête to slopers. Good fun, especially if you blow the last hard move.

❏ **7.** V7 SDS on two prominent sidepulls and climb the Bear Hug Arête.

❏ **8.** V1 Climb the triangular face between the two arêtes, not using either of them.

❏ **9.** V0 Arête that is a little slabby and insecure.

❏ **10.** VB Left side of the slab, starting at a right-facing sidepull and heading for the eyebrow feature above. Balancey and cool.

❏ **11.** VB Slab up the center of the face.

❏ **12.** VB Move up the slab into a subtle groove.

❏ **13.** VB Slab just left of the arête.

❏ **14.** VB Arête, also the downclimb for all the other problems.

❏ **15.** V2 Hard, crimpy first move at a seam.

Split Rock, Far Side

❏ **16.** V5 SDS on undercling and sidepull.

❏ **17.** V2 Start on the left-facing triangular sidepull.

❏ **18.** V4 Small right-facing sidepull into a shallow groove.

❏ **19.** V4 Crimps and sidepulls up a clean streak starting just left of the small rock in the corridor.

❏ **20.** V1 Climb the left side of the arête. Great quality moves.

❏ **21.** V1 Climb the right side of the arête to a challenging topout. Don't miss this one, and don't fall off it, either.

❏ **22.** V1 Start at 21, and traverse the seam right into 26. It's harder if you're short.

❏ **23. Project** V? Tiny edges and obscure sequences right of the arête problem. Looks hard.

❏ **24.** V1 Fun crack moves to insecure finish.

❏ **25. Project** V? Heinous, ridiculous slopers going up and left. Do this when it's ten below.

❏ **26.** V1 Edges and slopers to liebacking past a patch of moss.

❏ **27.** V1 Stand start and pull up onto the slab and it's over.

❏ **28. Physics Project** V11 SDS on the undercling start of 16, go left to a slopey rail and mantel the finish on 27. Another one for sub-zero conditions.

There is a cool V8 hueco problem with a sit start that is located 40 yards due west.

The Shadow Boulder

This blackish boulder sits about 100 yards south of Split Rock. It has a number of good and moderate high climbs mostly in the VB-V1 range.

❏ **1. V1** SDS on arête.

❏ **2. V3** Slaps and pinches on the white corner. Classic.

❏ **3. V?** Pocket with left hand, then toss for the moss.

❏ **4. V5** Squeeze the sidepulls just left of the brown circle, then take the arête edges.

❏ **5. V0** Start on edge in brown circle, then go right to seam.

❏ **6. VB** Stand on block and climb jugs.

❏ **7. VB** Undercling to seam.

❏ **8. V0** Flakes.

❏ **9. V1** Slopers on arête.

❏ **10. V4** Crimps to big throw. Height dependent.

❏ **11. V0** Left rising slopers on arête.

❏ **12. VB** Mossy diagonal crack.

❏ **13. V0** Jug to horizontal crack to mossy topout. Sloper landing.

❏ **14. V?** Climb the odd face in between the jug and the arête.

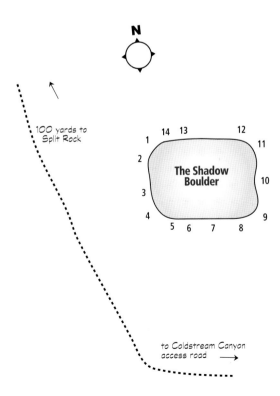

N

100 yards to Split Rock

The Shadow Boulder

14 13   12
1   11
2
                    10
3
4   9
5   6   7   8

to Coldstream Canyon access road →

Memorial Boulder

Approach time: **None**

Season: **March-December**

Number of problems: **19**

The Memorial Boulder's pretty funny. It's practically in the middle of town, and it's got a gazebo built right on top of it, with another little boulder fenced in inside it. It's kind of like a baby boulder in its crib – or maybe it's jailed so it can't get out and roll downtown for a beer. Whatever. It's a glacial erratic, deposited on top of the other boulder when some ancient slab of ice gave up the ghost and turned into the Truckee River. A local told me you used to be able to roll it around up there, but now there are shims under it – gotta keep these things under control, you know! The problems are pretty good, making this more than just a novelty. Unfortunately, the boulder is steadily getting shorter as the Veteran's Hall keeps repaving their parking lot. We should get them to excavate a little instead.

Driving Directions

Getting here's easy – you can see it from the highway and downtown both. From old downtown in Truckee (the touristy part) drive up Spring Street past a muddled five-way intersection and turn left on Keiser Street. You'll come up to the back of a Quonset hut type meeting hall, and the boulder's right there in front of you. Can't miss it, honest.

Approach

None.

Number of problems by difficulty

VB	V0	V1	V2	V3	V4	V5	V6	V7	V8	V9	V10	≥V11
1	2	1	2	2	1	1	6	1	0	0	1	1

Memorial Boulder

❏ **1. Superior Man** V7 SDS up the arch outside the dihedral right of the stairs.

❏ **2.** V4 Undercling start to small overhang. Also has a hard sit down start.

❏ **3. Fat Boy** V11 This problem has had no second ascent. Great-looking crimps to a sidepull with a hard exit.

❏ **4.** V7 Crank into a pair of gastons and head for the crimps.

❏ **5.** V3 Lieback the outside of this dihedral, and finish on Problem 4.

❏ **6.** V6 Start on a double-toothed hold right of the dihedral, and go for small edges up and right. Sweet sequence.

❏ **7. Project** V? Tiny crimps above the bushes.

❏ **8.** V10 SDS below a good left-facing sidepull to a slopey exit between two seams.

❏ **9.** V5 Jump start then left-facing sidepulls lead to a gray edge left of the crack.

❏ **10.** V3 Start just right of 9 on the same holds, but follow the crack up.

❏ **11.** VB Start just right of the bulging ledge and pull onto the small slab.

❏ **12.** V0 Start on a right trending seam, but go up, not right.

❏ **13.** V1 Traverse right on the seam to the end.

❏ **14.** V2 Slope and left-facing crimp to a dyno. Don't use the crack.

❏ **15.** V0 Start in the seam left of the stairs and go past a sidepull to a sloper.

❏ **16.** V2 Low start on good edges to a V slot, slopey top-out. Don't use the stairs.

Many other variations, eliminates and traverses have been done here.

Rainbow

Approach time: **1-5 minutes**

Season: **April-November**

Number of problems: **72**

Do you shop at 711, drive 100 mph everywhere, and curse the time it takes to microwave a burrito? If so, this is the place for you. Two and a half hours from the Bay Area will get you here, and the approach is minimal. Highway noise detracts a little from the ambience, but when you've just bailed out of cubicle-world in the city and need a burn so bad your hands are shaking, you won't even notice. The only thing that will filter through is sheer delight at being out bouldering in a great setting so soon after leaving work. Tiny amounts of hassle, big quantities of rock, and all the space in the world to run around in make Rainbow a sure thing.

The best time to climb is in the spring and fall. Right before the snow falls in November and Decemember (in a low snow year) is our favorite time to visit. In the summer, boulder in the mornings, then go find a more shaded bouldering area in the afternoons.

Driving Directions

On Interstate 80, just west of Kingvale, take the Rainbow exit. There are two concentations of boulders:

North side of 80 boulders
See the map.

South side of 80 boulders
From the bottom of the Interstate 80 off-ramp, drive one mile southwest and park in the big pullout on the right with the porta potty and info board. Now, backtrack for 100 feet and then start walking toward interstate 80. In just a hundred feet, you will reach a boulder with V4 undercut bulge, V3 southwest facing arête with room, and a V3 SDS problem. Walk another hundred feet and you will hit a boulder with a cool V3. Walk a little farther and you reach the main concentration that has an awesome V4 diagonal crack, a V1, a V6 arête (V8 SDS), and a marbley, funky, east-facing V11 bulge.

For the Sugar Cube, drive another few hundred feet past the main Rainbow parking and turn left onto a dirt road. Park immediately. Walk the road 100 feet southwest (pass a berm) until you reach a cabin on your left. The Sugar Cube is just to the right and has five cool problems rated V3, V3, V4, V6, and V7.

GPS Coordinates for North of Freeway

Second Parking Area: 38 18.765, 120 29.841
Monster Crack: 38 18.790, 120 29.983
Jawbone: 39 18.805, 120 30.014
The Patio: 39 18.798, 120 30.063

Number of problems by difficulty

VB	V0	V1	V2	V3	V4	V5	V6	V7	V8	V9	V10	≥V11
3	5	5	6	7	9	5	4	3	1	1	0	1

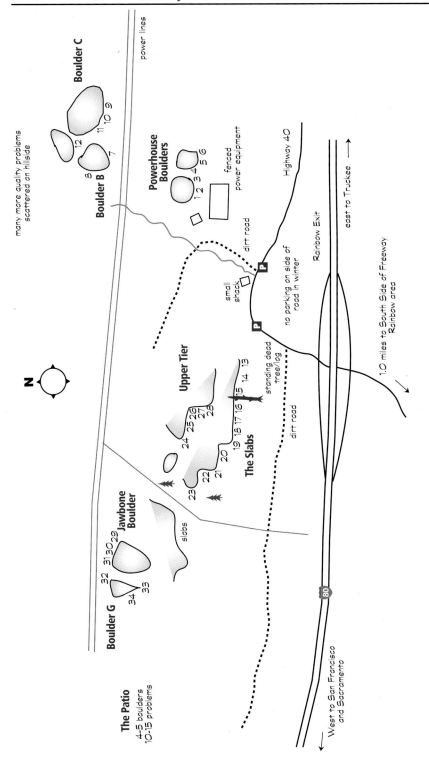

Rainbow - North side of Freeway

Boulder C

power lines

many more quality problems
scattered on hillside

Boulder B

12

8

7

9 10 11

Powerhouse
Boulders

1 2 3 4

5 6

fenced
power equipment

dirt road

N

small
shack

P

no parking on side of
road in winter

P

Highway 40

Rainbow Exit

east to Truckee

1.0 miles to South Side of Freeway
Rainbow area

Upper Tier

24 25 26
27
28

standing dead
tree/log

15 14 13
16
19 18 17

20

21

22

23

The Slabs

dirt road

Jawbone
Boulder

slabs

Boulder G

32 31 30 29

34 33

The Patio
4-5 boulders
10-15 problems

80

West to San Francisco
and Sacramento

Powerhouse Boulder

The biggest of the boulders just north of the fenced power station and shack.

❏ **1. Jam Master Jay V9** Super classic, super hard. Steep sidepulls to the striking 5.10 finger crack.

❏ **2. Project V?** This face is just right of Jam Master Jay.

❏ **3. Project V?** Another couple of high and hard face problems.

❏ **4. V?** Cave problem that faces west.

❏ **5. V?** SDS on edges to big slopers/shelves over bulge.

❏ **6. V?** Crack just right of tree.

Boulder B

Boulders B and C are a few hundred feet up the hill from the powef station.

❏ **7. Renegade Gonad V6** Striking high arête. Match hands on an edge, heel hook, then huge right hand move to edge. Finish up the arête (with your body on the left side). If you start off the boulder, the problem is V5.

❏ **8. Project V?** On the west west side of the boulder. Good gold edges to thin face.

Boulder C

❏ **9. V2** Start on a horizontal and climb the right-facing flake.

❏ **10. V3** Variation to 9 starting right of flake.

❏ **11. V4 Sidewinder** SDS on horizontal and follow crack up and left.

❏ **12. V1** Slab problem.

The Slabs

A number of problems on 8 to 20-foot tall tiered cliff bands just a few hundred feet

from the road. Problems 15-18 reference a dead tree that may have fallen over and be a log by the time you read this.

❏ **13. Kauk Slab V6** Classic thin slab that is harder and higher than it looks. Climb the distinct water streak right of a thin crack. More of a solo than a boulder problem.

❏ **14. V3** Thin crack.

❏ **15. Running Man V5** Just right of the dead tree. Get a running start, jump off a boulder and pull a stuntman move to snag the obvious hold.

❏ **16. V2** Start behind the dead tree with your left hand on a diagonal sloping edge. Move up to a small shelf.

❏ **17. V5** Balance problem. One foot starts on the boulder and then super balancey reaches get a right-facing edge.

❏ **18. V5** Start on tiny edges, then dyno up and right to big shelf.

❏ **19. V5** Rounded arête trending left to right.

❏ **20. Monster Crack V3** Classic high crack that diagonals right to left.

❏ **21. Project V?** Rounded arête with fragile holds.

❏ **22. VB** Finger and hand crack.

❏ **23. VB** Some short easy problems for kids.

Upper Tier

❏ **24. V4** SDS then follow the crack out a roof.

❏ **25. V6** Groove on orange rock to a hard and high face.

❏ **26. V4** Right-facing edge to thin face.

❏ **27.** V0 Finger to fist crack.

❏ **28.** V0 Left-leaning finger crack.

Jawbone Boulder

❏ **29. Mandible** V9 On the left side of the
north face, climb edges and sloping shelves
to a slab.

❏ **30. Jawbone** V7 The best problem at the
area. Climb the center of the north face on
steep edges to a high scary finish.

❏ **31. Project** V? Right side of this boulder.

Boulders G

The triangular boulder just west of Jawbone.

❏ **32.** V4 Short bulge on the north face.

❏ **33.** V2 Climb the long, high, and aesthetic
arête on the south side of the boulder.

❏ **34.** V1 Fun edging on the center of the
southwest face.

The Patio

A few hundred feet west of the Jawbone sit
a handful of glacial erratics on a large slab.
There are about 10-15 problems here.

The Firestones

This is a great concentration of 20 problems
in the V2-V11 range. It is also only two
hours from the Bay Area. From Sacramento,
drive 80 east to the Emigrant Gap exit.
Drive east on the road on the south side of
the freeway. At first the road is paved, then
it turns to dirt. Drive until you see the big
boulders. The south boulder has an amazing
V8 traverse called Ring of Fire. The other
boulders have a mega classic V11 called Big
Monster. There are a number of other classic
and more moderate problems.

Roadside Boulder A

❏ **1.** V4 SDS on prow on rounded holds.

❏ **2.** V0 Flake at head height. This is the downclimb for the other problems.

❏ **3.** V1 Large features right of Problem 2

❏ **4.** V? Heinous start on broken flake above low cave.

❏ **5.** V5 Pull on small features to sidepull above right side of overhang.

❏ **6.** V? Good edge just left of obvious runoff streak into hard dyno.

❏ **7.** V? SDS on arête by log.

❏ **8.** V? Footless tiny holds on barely overhanging wall.

Roadside Boulder B

❏ **9.** V2 Crack start, traverse right to left.

❏ **10.** V? Hard. Straight up tallest part of side. Step on bad left-hand sidepull.

❏ **11.** V5 Sloping rail to okay edges in scoop.

❏ **12.** V2 At end of rail, go up on slopers.

❏ **13.** VB Move over intersection of cracks.

❏ **14.** V0 Great right traverse to mantel finish.

❏ **15.** V4 Bad, polished slopers to sharp, tiny edges.

Roadside Boulder C

❏ **22.** V3 Obvious dyno in center of wall.

❏ **16.** V? Knobs to horizontal crack.

❏ **17.** V7 Tiny nubbins to slab above passage under boulder.

❏ **18.** V? Knobby and slopey Tuolumne-style arête.

❏ **19.** V2 Up problem in center of traverse.

❏ **20.** V3 Awesome traverse crack. Classic.

❏ **21.** V3 At right end of traverse, go up.

Roadside Boulder D

❏ **22.** V3 Obvious dyno in center of wall.

❏ **23.** V2 Start at right side of rail and finish up and right.

❏ **24.** V? Ungodly sit start, up right of arête.

❏ **25.** V? Hard slopers on licheny face 15 feet right of Problem 24.

❏ **26.** V? Bleak sidepulls to pinch slopers eight feet right of Problem 25.

❏ **27. Pocket Project** V? Small left-hand sidepull and suspect pocket to edge.

❏ **28.** V11 Horrendous right-facing undercling to tiny knobs above small cave.

❏ **29.** V? Jump start to good edge, go up and right through a series of edges.

❏ **30.** V1 Edge and traingle flake, to jugs eight feet right of cedar tree.

❏ **31.** V? Identical crescent moon flakes. One move to big edge.

The Sugar Cube (Yosemite Boulder)

❏ **1.** V4 Awkward pinch start to traverse left.

❏ **2.** V5 Highball up scoop.

❏ **3.** V3 Arête on northeast side of boulder.

❏ **4. Sweet N Low** V7 Steep start. Big horizontal rail to hard arête.

❏ **5. Sweet N Low Traverse** V6 Start on problem 4 and finish on problem 1.

❏ **6.** V0 Crack.

❏ **7.** V1 Crack.

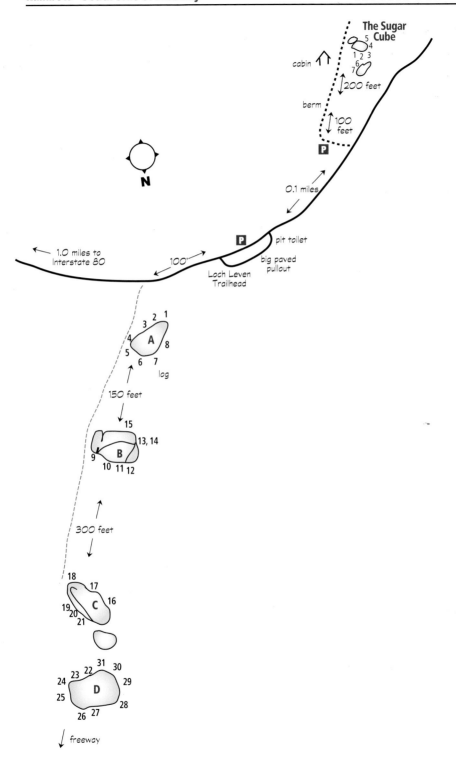

The Sugar Cube

cabin

berm

200 feet

100 feet

P

0.1 miles

N

P   pit toilet

1.0 miles to Interstate 80

100'   big paved pullout

Loch Leven Trailhead

2 1
3
A   8
4
5   6 7
log

150 feet

15
13, 14
9   B
10 11 12

300 feet

18
17
16
19 20 C
21

31 30
23 22
24   29
25   D
26 27 28

freeway

Washoe Boulders

Approach time: **4 minutes**

Season: **year round**

Number of problems: **60+**

Rusted out car frames, flea-ridden fixed mattresses, shotgun shells, broken glass, and the steady pop-pop-pop of small arms fire make the Washoe Boulders an unforgettable experience. The backdrop of a massive black cinder mine completes the surreal, industrial vibe, which is tempered by stunning views of the surrounding mountain ranges.

If you can make it past the casinos in downtown Carson City with enough money left to buy chalk, you'll love the bouldering.

There isn't a speck of granite worth pulling on for ten miles in any direction, which is great. After too many days in the basin, it feels good to grab some pocketed volcanic stone instead of cerebral Sierra granite.

The Washoe Boulders reward power and a high pain threshold. The pockets and edges here are incredibly sharp, so taping ahead of time might give you a shot at climbing here two days in a row, but no guarantees.

Chris McNamara on Wasabi.

Driving Directions

Getting here isn't too bad. From Tahoe, take Highway 50 into Carson City, turn north on Highway 395, drive all the way through town to College Parkway and turn right. It's farther than you think, and the last light on the north end of town.

From Reno, take 395 south towards Carson and turn left on College Parkway - the first light as you come into town.

Follow College Parkway to Goni Road. Turn left at the light just before a Sonic Burger and follow Goni out into the hills. At

one point it'll break hard right just in front of a quarry. That means you're on track. Stay on Goni until it makes a right-hand switchback in front of a black cinder mine where the tailings come all the way down to the road. Park well out of the way on the left, because some huge trucks occasionally come through here.

Approach

You'll be parked right in front of a dirt road blocked by a boulder—that's the goods. Follow it to the first junction, stay right, and head past the dead car chassis towards the boulders. You'll probably walk in near the impressive main wall.

Kevin Swift on problem 19.

Number of problems by difficulty

VB	V0	V1	V2	V3	V4	V5	V6	V7	V8	V9	V10	≥V11
10	6	7	22	9	3	4	2	1	0	1	0	0

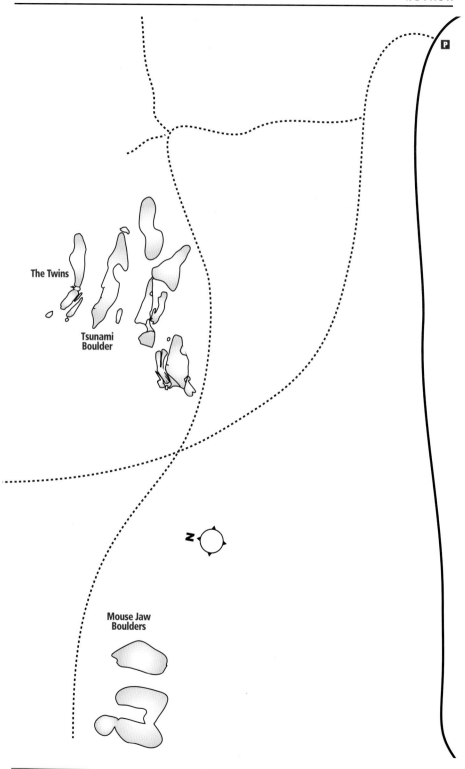

The Twins

Tsunami
Boulder

N

Mouse Jaw
Boulders

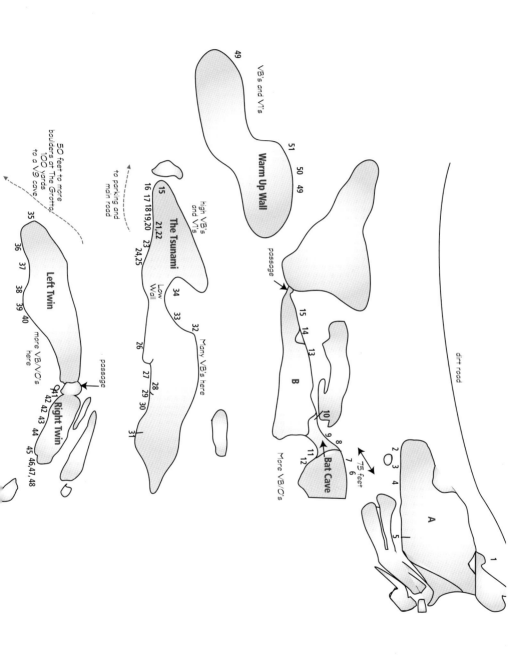

Warm Up Wall

VB's and V1's

49

50 49

51

49

passage

The Tsunami

high VB's and V1's

15
16 17 18 19,20
21,22
23
24,25

Low Wall

34

33

32

Many VB's here

26

27 28
29 30
31

to parking and main road

50 feet to more boulders at The Grotto; 100 yards to a V9 cave.

Left Twin

35
36
37
38
39 40

more VB/VO's here

passage

41
42 42 43
44
45 46,47,48

Right Twin

B

15
14
13

10

9
8
11
12

Bat Cave

7 6

75 feet

2
3
4

5

A

1

More VB/VO's

dirt road

Boulder A

This wall isn't that visually stimulating, but the problems are okay. Just watch the uncertain rock and bad landing on 5 and 6.

❏ **1. Storm Cycle V5** Start on lieback at far left of cave. Work out right through holds under prow. Finish on jugs on the right side of prow.

❏ **2. V0** Edges and good holds on the left side of the boulder.

❏ **3. V1** Slightly harder than Problem 1.

❏ **4. V0** More edges and holds. Good warm-up.

❏ **5. V2** SDS in the cave to a tall crack problem with a weird landing. Okay moves, but the crack needs cleaning.

Boulder B

There are some odd little problems in the cave/passageway you can see from the road. The rock looks worse than it is, and some of the moves are pretty entertaining.

❏ **6. VB** Big buckets lead up a short face left of the cave.

❏ **7. V0** SDS on the left side of the passage at huge holds.

❏ **8. Cave Out V2** Start on a friable hanging flake (it's still there, right?) and finish up the crack.

❏ **9. Jason Lives V3** SDS at a good undercling right of the passage, then up and slightly left.

❏ **10. V2** Start just right of 9 and finish up and right on pockets.

❏ **11. Cave In V2** Start on the same creaky flake as 8, but go through the passage and finish up jugs on the opposite aspect from the other problems. Thuggish fun.

❏ **12. VB** Climb the big holds climber's right of the passage.

❏ **13. Eye of The Hawk V3** Start five feet left of Twister and work right on lip of cave.

❏ **14. Twister V3** SDS on a left-facing sloper and crank up and right to sloper to pockets.

❏ **15. Arch Enemy V4** From huge crunchy jug, reach out to lip.

Tsunami, North Face

The main wall is long, tall, and steeply overhung, allowing climbing here in all but the worst weather. All the problems on the left side of this formation are tall, hard, and proud—the best Washoes have.

❏ **15. Convergence** V1
Same start as Mountaineers Route but move up and left. Wild and juggy.

❏ **16. Mountaineers Route**
V2 Start at the large crack littered with jugs, then crank as high as you dare, watching the pad turn into a matchbook before your eyes. The end isn't that hard, but keep your head up because the lichen can be treacherous.

❏ **17. Little Japanese Village** V5 SDS three feet right of 16, start with your left hand in a big hole/dish. Second move crux, followed by easier pulls above. Don't escape to the crack until you've passed the bulge. Future sick finish right.

❏ **18. Wasabi** V7 SDS at low pockets just left of a diagonal, sloping rail that you can use for an alternate SDS at the same grade. Pull into an obvious series of three great pockets eight feet up, getting the first right-handed, and stay left of the crack all the way up, hitting a crux near the top. For a variation, start on 18 but hit the pocket with your left hand and go right to the edge of a slot, catch a small undercling and dyno to a sharp pocket by the crack. Finish on 19.

❏ **19.** V6 SDS and climb the left-leaning crack.

❏ **20. Alcatraz** V3 SDS under the crack on 19 but move up and right from jug to jug.

❏ **21. Escape From Alcatraz** V3 Do the crux bulge of Alcatraz, then escape right.

❏ **22.** V3 Start on 21 and traverse out right under the bulge, then move up.

❏ **23. Back to the Slammer** V2 SDS. Ledgy rail move up and right. Then move back left to Escape from Alcatraz.

❏ **24. Birdman** V1 SDS on small edges and go up and right over the bulge.

❏ **25.** V5 Traverse from 24 to 15 at chest height and finish on 15.

Tsunami, North Face (cont'd)

❏ **26. Jump** V5 SDS at a pointy undercling and an edge, then pull through small pockets. Short but cool.

❏ **27.** VB Crack/dihedral problem.

❏ **28. Silver Surfer** V0 SDS at a triangle slot, then climb straight up left of the crack.

❏ **29.** V2 Two diverging seams lead the way, encouraging bad crack technique by having so many features to work with.

❏ **30. Catch and Release** V1 Low start on two great pockets to edges and a slab.

❏ **31.** VB Follow the yellow brick... seam/crack thingy.

Tsunami , South Face (not shown)

The next three problems are on the opposite side of this formation.

❏ **32.** V2 SDS in the back of a tiny cave on a big sidepull and crank over the lip. Height dependent, also short and pointless.

❏ **33. Name** V2 SDS on the right side of the overhang on small holds just left of the slab, then go to the jug and mantel.

❏ **35. Swing Shift** V2 Start left and traverse up and right at lip of cave.

Frank Lucido on Was

Left Twin

The next wall east of the passage has a few okay problems uphill, and some cleaning might yield others. No photo.

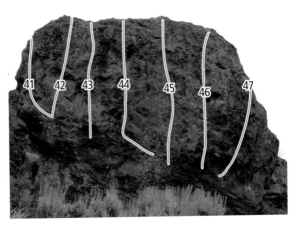

☐ **35.** VB Short sharp arête that needs cleaning.

☐ **36. Baco Bits** VB Start at a good two-finger pocket and go to jugs. Taller and more fun than 35.

☐ **37.** VB Climb a right-facing seam/feature.

☐ **38.** VB Pull over a tiny bulge to a big pocket streaked with guano.

☐ **39. Sizzleen** VB Undercling to licheny holds on a low bulge. Needs cleaning.

☐ **40. Traverse Al-Qaeda's Monkey Bars** V2 Traverse entire face from right to left.

Right Twin

☐ **41. The Prow** V2 SDS just right of the prow at the passageway. Climb sidepulls to pockets and a horn on steep rock.

☐ **42. Dyno-Saur** V2 SDS at the guano-covered edge, go up and right past a gaston to the right side of the tiny roof.

☐ **43. Short White Men Can't Jump** V2 Height-dependent edging.

☐ **44. Maggot Brain** V2 Low start with your right hand in a slot and your left on a pinch in the center of the wall and finish as 41.

☐ **45. Crescent Moon Direct** V3 A few different starts. Move up through arch.

☐ **46. Chad 5** V2 Start at diagonal slot. Move up and left.

☐ **46. Chad's Arête** V2 Low start with your

right hand in a slopey pocket. Stay left of the arête as you climb.

☐ **47. Dihedral** V1 Same start to cool, tricky moves in a dihedral.

☐ **46. The Few The Prowed** V2 SDS below the bulge, slap and sidepull your way to a mantel finish.

☐ **47. Cozy Hang** V4

☐ **48.** V4 Traverse entire face.

Warm Up Wall

☐ **49. Grand Traverse** V1 100-foot traverse left to right at head level.

☐ **50. C4** V3 Start on triangular-shaped hold. Pop up right to crimp.

☐ **51. Pop the Clutch Jane** V1 Low start. Climb up and right through pockets.

The Grotto

Walk 50 feet north of The Tsunami, you run into a jumble of boulders. There are a few classics in the corridors. Continue walking north down the hill for the V9 cave. This is a wicked horizontal problem.

Mouse Jaw Boulders

☐ **1. Lip Service** V?

☐ **2. The Ant and The Elephant** V6 Start on guano-covered two-handed edge at base of prow. Reach left, then go up.

☐ **3. Mouse or Man** V2 SDS five feet left of 2. Go up right side of crack.

☐ **4. Mouse Jam Crack** VB Dirty.

☐ **5. Bump and Run** V2 SDS with left hand on arête. Work through pockets. Jump for big red lip.

☐ **6. Speed Bump** V0 Go up arête.

☐ **7. Side Salad No Dressing** V3 Start on right-facing lieback. Work up left on diagonal arête.

☐ **8. Dr. Amorphous** V3 Crack to cool summit gendarme.

☐ **9. Mantel Shelf** V2 Mantel.

☐ **10. Cork Screw** V0 Guano holds.

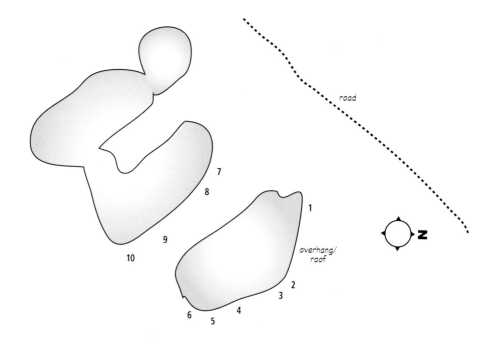

North of Reno

There are a number of winter bouldering areas 30 minutes to 1.5 hours north of Reno. The rock ranges from Joshua Tree-style granite to volcanic and metamorphic rocks. Visit these areas from October-April.

Purgatory

Purgatory has over 200 established problems with rock quality similar to the best of Joshua Tree. The rock is featured, sharp, and clean with very little grit. There are hundreds more problems to establish here.

Purgatory is about 1.5 hours north of Reno. Before heading out of Reno, top off your gas tank. There is no reliable source of gas once you are in the desert. From Reno, follow Highway 80 to Pyramid Way, Highway 445, and follow it to Pyramid Lake. Turn right on Highway 446 and take it to Nixon.

Once you have found the Nixon Store (recently closed) follow Highway 447 north for 41 miles. When you pass the north shore of the dry Winnemucca Lake, find (at 41 miles from Nixon Store) the obvious large dirt road following the large power line. Turn right and follow the road east toward the prominent craggy peaks for one mile. Turn left onto a small dirt road and find your way to the boulder field, which is now easily seen below the peaks. There are north and south parking areas at the dead ends of small spur roads.

Family Boulders

Amidst jumbled and broken volcanic rock there are several good faces. There are about 30 sharp and quality problems here.

Take Highway 80 to Wadsworth exit 43. At the first stop sign turn left onto Highway 447 and travel north on Highway 447 about 2.4 miles to a gigantic dirt road, which cuts through the desert on your left. Follow this three miles to a corral on the right. Turn right and make a hairpin turn onto a faint dirt road. Backtrack down this road and you will find these volcanic boulders.

Page 180: Ludde Hagberg at Middle Bliss. Photo by Chris McNamara.
Page 181: Chris McNamara at Middle Bliss. Photo by Ludde Hagberg.
Page 182: Mark Nicholas at the Deli Slicer.